hamlyn

FOOD BOOSTERS
for Kids

Amanda Cross

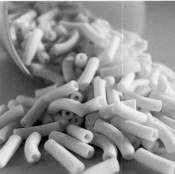

First published in Great Britain in 2002 by Hamlyn,
a division of Octopus Publishing Group Limited,
2–4 Heron Quays, London E14 4JP

ISBN 0 600 60420 9

A CIP catalogue record for this book is available from the British
Library

Printed and bound in China

10 9 8 7 6 5 4 3 2 1

Notes

Standard level spoon measurements are used in all recipes.
1 tablespoon = one 15 ml spoon
1 teaspoon = one 5 ml spoon

Both metric and imperial measurements are given for the recipes.
Use one set of measurements only, not a mixture of both.

Fresh herbs should be used unless otherwise stated. If
unavailable, use dried herbs as an alternative but halve the
quantities stated.

Pepper should be freshly ground black pepper unless otherwise
stated.

Ovens should be preheated to the specified temperature. If using
a fan-assisted oven, follow the manufacturer's instructions for
adjusting the time and temperature. Grills should also be
preheated.

This book includes dishes made with nuts and nut derivatives.
Anyone with a known nut allergy must avoid these. It is also
prudent to check the labels of pre-prepared ingredients for the
possible inclusion of nut derivatives. Children under the age of 3
with a family history of nut allergy, asthma, eczema or any other
type of allergy are also advised to avoid eating dishes which
contain nuts. Do not give whole nuts or seeds to any child under 5
because of the risk of choking.

The information given in this book should not be considered as a
replacement for professional medical treatment; a physician should
be consulted in all matters relating to health and especially in
relation to any symptoms which may require diagnosis or medical
attention. While the advice and information in this book is believed
to be accurate, neither the author nor publisher can accept any
legal responsibility for any injury or illness sustained while following
the advice given.

CONTENTS

INTRODUCTION

Your children trust you. They count on you to help them with their homework, and when they get hurt, you are the first one they run to. They also entrust you with their health and nutrition. It is part of your job to ensure they are eating a healthy, balanced diet that provides everything the growing body needs. This could make the difference between a lifetime of low energy and poor health, and one of vitality and well-being. Sadly, many parents in the western world are letting their children down.

Strange as it may seem, many children today have a poorer diet than their predecessors in the post-war period. Recent reports based on diet and nutrition surveys in the USA and UK have revealed that most children between the ages of four and 18 are eating a diet dominated by junk food loaded with fat, sugar, artificial colour, sweeteners and flavours. The statistics are startling:

★ According to a recent survey by the Food Standards Agency and the Department of Health, children in the UK eat four times as many biscuits as portions of leafy green vegetables and drink two-thirds more fizzy drinks than milk or water.
★ In the USA, the rate of obesity keeps rising, yet 30 per cent of children are actually malnourished. Although poverty is obviously a contributory factor in this, dietary ignorance cannot be discounted.

★ The majority of those surveyed consume less than half the recommended five portions of fruit and vegetables per day.

These nutritional deficiencies and poor eating habits predispose children to learning and behavioural problems, recurring colds and flu, and also chronic conditions that will impair their quality of life and possibly shorten it. After all, eating habits established in childhood will tend to continue throughout a person's life. In fact, evidence indicates that of the top ten causes of death, five are attributable, at least in part, to dietary habits formed in childhood.

A healthy, well-nourished child has a strong immune system that will help to ward off infections and disease. However, according to a report released by the UK Office for National Statistics in June 2000:

★ One in five young people aged between 16 and 24 reported long-term illnesses in 1998–9.
★ Around 4.5 million prescriptions for antibiotics were written for the under-16s in 1998.
★ One in four children suffer from allergies and food intolerances.

Even more alarmingly, cancer rates in the under-20s have risen dramatically. The Cancer Research

All the recipes in this book have been coded to let you know at a glance whether they are suitable for your child:

 vegan

 egg-free

 vegetarian

 dairy-free

 gluten-free

 can be frozen

wheat-free

Campaign figures estimate a rise of around 27 per cent since 1971.

Can a poor diet be held responsible for this meltdown in our children's health? Perhaps not entirely, but it is certainly a major contributor, along with lack of exercise, environmental pollution, overuse of antibiotics and other drugs, and genetic predisposition.

By providing a diet abundant in natural goodness you can give your children the best possible chance of growing up fit and healthy, strengthening their immunity against infection and reducing the possibility of chronic disease in later life.

IS IT EVER TOO LATE TO START?

No. Chuck out the junk. Fill your refrigerator and cupboards with healthy alternatives. It may not be as difficult as you think. Tasty meals and snacks can be made using inexpensive and easily obtained ingredients without additives and preservatives. Using the recipes and suggestions in this book, you can make a start and you will probably see a positive difference almost immediately. If you want to boost your children's immune system, brainpower, energy levels, growth and development, then their diet is the best place to start, and the sooner the better.

HOW TO USE THIS BOOK

With its nutritious recipes and guidelines for a balanced diet, this book is designed to inspire you to boost your children's health. I have included a mixture of dishes that will appeal to your children, and will also slot into any family mealtime. I stress the importance of seeking organic, natural food and, rather than labour the point in every recipe, I suggest you remember the following guidelines:

★ Use organic fruit and vegetables where possible; alternatively, make sure that all fruits and vegetables are thoroughly washed or peeled before use.

★ Use organic wholemeal flour in the recipes, or a wheat-free/gluten-free alternative if your child has a wheat and/or gluten intolerance.

★ Use free-range, organic eggs.

★ I have used either oil or butter in the recipes, but if you do have to use margarine, make sure it is unhydrogenated.

★ Salt and pepper are always mentioned as optional; if using, keep them moderate.

★ Whenever milk is used in a recipe, you can always opt for a non-dairy alternative such as soya or almond milk, or try goats' milk, which is much safer for children with a lactose intolerance.

MALNUTRITION

If I asked you if your child was suffering from malnutrition, you would probably look at me in amazement and say that your child eats well and is not underweight. But I am not talking about starvation. Malnutrition is a specific condition caused by an imbalance between what a body needs and what it actually consumes to maintain health. This can lead to a number of common diseases that develop gradually after years of eating foods that do not provide the necessary combination of the major nutrients, vitamins, minerals and trace elements.

In today's high-pressured, hectic world, we seem to have lost the concept of perfect health and well-being. Many children are suffering and having their future health put at risk because their parents and even their health care providers are not giving enough emphasis to a well-balanced diet as a means of preventing infection and disease.

WHAT ARE THE MAIN CONTRIBUTORY FACTORS?

There are two principal causes of malnutrition: the quality of the food we eat and the lifestyle we lead.

Poor-quality food
In an ideal world, the food we eat should be able to supply us with everything we need to keep us

Below: Like all citrus fruits, lemons are rich in vitamin C. Although sour, they have many uses in cooking.

SIGNS OF MALNUTRITION

★ Dark hollowed eyes ★ Cracks around the mouth ★ White marks on the nails ★ Tooth decay ★ Digestive problems such as constipation, diarrhoea or flatulence ★ Hyperactivity and restlessness ★ Fatigue or apathy ★ Dull hair and blotchy or excessively dry skin ★ Stunted growth ★ Continual runny nose and catarrh

Malnutrition is a specific condition caused by an imbalance between what a body needs and what it actually consumes to maintain health.

healthy, but in the modern western world this is becoming increasingly difficult due to a combination of factors:

★ The quality of the soil in which our food is grown has been damaged over the years through intensive farming, leading to a diminished source of essential minerals.

★ As consumers we demand a ready supply of perfect-looking produce all year round. This means that supermarkets are selling us food that has been treated with chemical additives to make it look more attractive and prolong its shelf life. Unfortunately, this decreases the vitamin and mineral content of the food and, to make matters worse, pumps us full of toxins.

★ The food industry often cuts the nutrient value of foods through processing, preserving, canning, freezing, drying and storing. When you consider that white flour and refined sugar lose virtually all their nutritional benefit during processing, it does seem a high price to pay. Nevertheless, we carry on filling our trolleys with products made up primarily of those two ingredients. Check the label on your child's sugary breakfast cereal and prepare yourself for a shock. Even if it claims to be fortified, you can be sure that the manufacturer has taken out more than they put back in.

★ Lean meat is a valuable source of complete protein and vitamin B12, but it is seen by many nutritionists as a highly contaminated food source. In the search for higher profits the livestock industry has used force-feeding, drugs, hormones, antibiotics and tranquillizers to speed up growth and increase weight. The meat you are feeding your children, particularly if it is highly processed (for example burgers and sausages), is probably laden with toxins.

Below: Many ingredients lose much of their nutritional value through being processed and refined. White flour and white sugar are two such examples.

Lifestyle

Children today tend to lead a far more sedentary lifestyle than their predecessors. They seem to prefer staying indoors, playing video games, surfing the net or sitting glued to the television, rather than getting fresh air and exercise outdoors. Unfortunately, a life indoors denies a child's body the natural surge of energy provided by the endorphins, a group of chemicals produced by the body in response to exercise. This makes the body rely on the stimulation provided by eating junk food instead. A lack of exercise can also have a disastrous effect on growth and development by lowering the metabolic rate and reducing the ratio of muscle to body fat, sometimes resulting in obesity.

If children are eating most of their meals in front of the television, then the chances are that they are not concentrating on what they are eating. One has to be aware that digestion begins in the mouth, and if children are failing to chew their food properly, then the enzyme salivary amylase does not get the opportunity it needs to start breaking down the starch. This essentially means that fewer of the vital energy-giving carbohydrates will be absorbed effectively into the bloodstream, which can result in fatigue and lethargy.

Filling the kids with convenience foods and snacks has become a way of life for parents with busy lifestyles, but these highly processed foods are full of additives, saturated fats, sugar and salt, and they are often addictive.

Parents inevitably pass on their own food fads and phobias to their children. They may be obsessive about dieting and all things low-fat, for example, or they may follow a particular dietary regime for other reasons. This may not necessarily correspond with a healthy diet for a child, who needs a good balance of all the essential nutrients in order to grow and

Below: Sedentary pursuits such as computer games should be balanced by sufficient fresh air and exercise.

A life indoors denies a child's body the natural surge of energy provided by the endorphins, a group of chemicals produced by the body in response to exercise.

develop. Similarly, many vegetarians and vegans also restrict their children's diets in accordance with their own, but they may not be ensuring that their child is getting the full complement of nutrients they need to remain healthy.

HOW CAN MALNUTRITION LEAD TO DISEASE?

Prolonged nutritional deficiencies can lead to the development of toxaemia in the body. This essentially means that the body is less efficient at excreting its waste products, so they build up and gradually contaminate the body, weakening the immune system. In this environment, disease-causing (pathogenic) bacteria and viruses can flourish. Tonsillitis is a good example: the tonsils become inflamed and enlarged in an attempt to rid the body of toxins, allergens or microbes that gain a foothold due to the failure of the body's immune system to keep them at bay. This is unlikely to happen in a healthy, strong body.

If a child does not take in sufficient antioxidant vitamins, then the body can accumulate highly reactive free radicals, which can lead to degenerative diseases such as cancer and high blood pressure. Our nervous systems also need a range of specific vitamins, minerals and amino acids to function properly. If these are lacking, the body chemistry can be disturbed, causing negativity and anxiety. This is another factor that can weaken the immune system and leave the body more prone to infection.

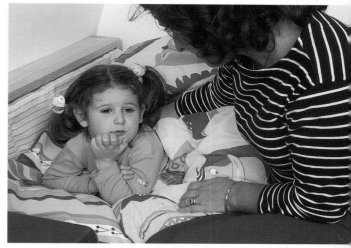

Above: Poor nutrition leads to a weakened immune system and consequent proneness to recurring illness.

Even though congenital or hereditary conditions such as diabetes or certain allergies are not caused by a nutritional deficiency, the symptoms will be magnified if there is a nutritional imbalance. Conversely, they can be modified by a well-balanced diet and the correct supplements.

In addition, there are a whole host of diseases that are directly caused by nutritional deficiencies. In the past, conditions such as scurvy (lack of vitamin C) and anaemia (lack of vitamin B12) were fatal; now we suffer from milder forms of such conditions that sometimes go undetected as the symptoms are not so severe. Watching out for some of the symptoms of malnutrition listed earlier and seeking nutritional advice are vital if you want to help your children achieve optimum health through a balanced diet.

What's wrong with
JUNK FOOD?

Above: Fizzy drinks are loaded with sugar, which is as much of a treat for the germs that cause tooth decay and stomach upsets as it is for your child.

Junk foods, such as cakes, pastries, crisps, sweets and carbonated drinks, are laden with refined sugar and flour, saturated fats, salt and additives, all of which are detrimental to your child's health. As has been shown, a diet based on these foods can lead to attention deficit disorder, compromised immune system functioning and habits that will lead children to a lifetime of obesity, disease and disability. Most

junk foods give children an initial lift, but then they let them down and this can lead to depression and mood swings. There is an undeniable link between poor diet and poor performance.

Consider just a few of the risks:

★ Refined sugars promote cavity-causing bacteria in the mouth and, if consumed in large quantities, can put a strain on the liver by raising blood sugar to abnormally high levels.
★ A diet high in saturated fats and refined sugars can lead to obesity.
★ A high sodium intake may lead to high blood pressure, particularly if hypertension runs in the family.
★ Cured, smoked and charred foods, artificial sweeteners, dyes and other additives have all been linked to an increased risk of cancer.

TOP FIVE NUTRI NO-NOS

1 *Refined sugar*

When scientists in a laboratory want to cultivate a few germs in a dish, what do they put in to aid growth? Yes, you've guessed it – sugar. Germs just love it – all the bacteria responsible for tooth decay, stomach upsets, meningitis and more have a particular fondness for sugar. And so does yeast. We all have yeast present in our bodies and generally it does no harm, but as soon as it is fed with an excess of sugar, it produces a toxin that can be detrimental to our health, particularly to our reproductive, nervous and digestive systems.

And yet children are eating loads of sugar, because food manufacturers put huge amounts into products aimed at children, even into baby food. According to nutritionist and author Bernard Jensen, in 1900 Americans consumed on average 4.5 kg (10 lb) of sugar per person per year. By 1983, that figure had risen to an amazing 60 kg (130 lb) per person per year.

One of the key things to remember about white sugar is that it depletes the body of vital nutrients, namely some of the B vitamins and the minerals zinc and chromium. Sugar needs these to be metabolized by the body. Natural unrefined sugar contains these components, but the refining process takes them away. So when children eat excessive amounts of white sugar, their bodies have to secrete these vitamins and minerals in order to digest it.

Another problem caused by refined sugar is that the body has to produce more insulin to cope with it. This can trigger diabetes and hypoglycaemia. Large secretions of insulin can also inhibit growth hormone, which is essential to a child's healthy growth and development.

Above: Some salt is essential but too much strains young kidneys and can cause health problems later on.

2 Salt

Sodium chloride, commonly known as salt, occurs naturally in foods, usually in small amounts, but most dietary sodium comes from foods to which salt has been added during processing or preparation. Potato chips, savoury snacks, smoked foods, processed foods, even breakfast cereals are all very salt rich.

Although sodium plays an essential role in the body, regulating fluids and blood pressure, many studies have shown that a high sodium intake is associated with high blood pressure. Recent research

carried out in The Netherlands suggests that babies and infants given a low-sodium diet run a lower risk of high blood pressure and cardiac problems later in life.

Another reason to limit a child's salt intake is the fact that a salt-rich diet may increase the amount of calcium excreted in the urine, reducing the levels of this essential mineral available for growth. Excessive sodium intake also puts the kidneys under pressure and depletes the body's magnesium, which is needed for the immune system to function normally.

3 *Hydrogenated fat*

Hydrogenated fat is solid or semi-solid at room temperatures. The best example of this is margarine. Hydrogenated fats are created when a liquid oil that is largely unsaturated, such as corn oil, has hydrogen added to it, changing its chemical structure. Hydrogenated oils have the same capacity to do harm as saturated fats. In fact they interfere with the metabolism of some essential fatty acids. Research has shown the *trans* fatty acids in hydrogenated fats can increase the LDL (bad) cholesterol, decrease the HDL (good) cholesterol and thus increase the risk of coronary heart disease.

Hydrogenated fats are found in almost every processed food in the supermarket, from soups to fries, crackers to cookies, pastries to some pasta and rice mixes. They are also found in frozen foods such as pizza and ready meals, and even some cereals. When you order deep-fried foods – doughnuts, French fries, chicken, fish, and so on – remember that hydrogenated fats are often used to fry them.

4 *Caffeine*

Some people are surprised to learn that children are increasingly addicted to caffeine. Remember that caffeine does not appear only in the form of coffee; high levels are also found in most carbonated drinks, in chocolate and in tea.

Recent research by the US Department of Agriculture revealed that children and teenagers in the USA are guzzling more than 300 litres (64 gallons) of fizzy drink a year. This amount has tripled for teenagers since 1978, doubled for the six to 11-year age group and increased by a quarter for tots younger than five. These caffeine-loaded fizzy drinks can pack a wallop equivalent to three cups of strong coffee and are bombarding a body that may be only half to two-thirds the size of an adult.

The effects that caffeine can have on the body and on behaviour are well known. A low dose may aid concentration and task completion in an adult, but higher doses typically make children nervous, anxious, fidgety, frustrated and quicker to anger. Such symptoms can easily be misdiagnosed as attention deficit disorder with hyperactivity (see page 62). Like adults, children who regularly drink caffeine suffer ill effects when they do not get a regular shot. They will eventually become dependent on caffeine.

Caffeine can also be harmful to growth. Large doses cause excessive excretion of calcium and magnesium, vital elements for the formation of a normal bone mass. This is exacerbated by the fact that children are now less likely to drink milk as part of their daily diet.

Left and right: French fries, chocolate and fizzy drinks should all be occasional treats rather than the mainstay of your children's diet. The effects of caffeine, salt, fat and sugar, noticeable in adults, are profound in the smaller body of a child.

It is feared that many potential problems related to excessive caffeine consumption in childhood will not be seen until the children mature. For example, there may be increasing rates of osteoporosis as well as hypertension.

Experts recommend that for children and teens their intake should stay well under 100 mg of caffeine per day. This is equivalent to between one and two cans of fizzy drink (depending on the caffeine content).

5 Additives

The jury is out on food additives. It would appear that as far as the food industry is concerned, we cannot live without them, but for certain groups, such as asthmatics, people allergic to aspirin and hyperactive children, the side effects can be devastating. The symptoms seen in sensitive people can include skin rashes, fever, blurred vision, hay fever, stomach upsets, breathlessness, nausea, dizziness, headaches, palpitations and extreme behaviour.

Food additives are designed to make food look good, taste better and have a longer shelf life, and they are abundant in all processed foods. Even foods that should be classified as fresh, such as fruit and vegetables, have often been sprayed with chemicals to preserve their freshness. But what effect does this have on your children's livers, which have to work overtime to get rid of all the toxins?

Although certain additives are banned from foods and drinks aimed at babies and young children, they are so commonly used in other foods it is difficult to ensure that even the smallest child does not consume them in some form or another. Packets of potato chips, chicken nuggets, carbonated drinks, sweets – all contain additives and only the most careful parent manages to shield their small child completely from such products.

All processed food must list the ingredients clearly on the packaging. This includes additives, which are listed under their code number. Whenever you see a number preceded with an 'E', this means it has been approved for use by the European Union, those with no 'E' are only allowed in the UK. Additives that have been approved by the Food and Drug Administration in the United States are preceded with 'FD&C'.

If your child has a problem with food additives it is vital that you check all ingredient listings for the offending numbers. An older child can even be given a list so that they can check for themselves when out of your care.

Ideally, it would be best to ditch all processed food and opt for a natural wholefood lifestyle. But if wiping convenience foods totally from your shopping basket is not really an option, check out the list overleaf, which shows the most widely used food additives and the products in which they are usually found.

Common food
ADDITIVES

E102 Tartrazine/107 Yellow 2G ▲▼★

Yellow/orange colour widely used in drinks, cakes, biscuits, puddings, meat products, smoked cod and haddock, sauces, confectionery and snacks.

E110 Sunset yellow ▲★

Yellow colour used in chocolate drinks, packet soups and desserts, biscuits, breadcrumbs and preserves.

E120 Cochineal ▲

Natural red colour from dried insects and egg yolk. There is a synthetic version. Both used in confectionery and cakes.

E122 Carmoisine ▲▼★

Reddish-purple colour used in raspberry drinks, jam, desserts and sauces, brown sauces and packet soups.

E123 Amaranth ▲★

Red colour used in drinks, fruit pie fillings, jellies, cakes, puddings, packet soups, gravy mixes and beefburgers.

E124 Poncea ▲▼★

Red colour used in meat pastes, tomato soup, strawberry products – pie fillings, jellies, puddings – and cake mixes.

E127 Erythrosine ▲

Red colour used in glacé cherries, canned fruits, packet desserts, biscuits, ham and pork products and some potato snacks. It is also used in tablets to reveal plaque on teeth.

128 Red 2G ▲

Red colour used in pork pies, sausages and other meat products.

E131 Patent blue V ▲▼★●

Violet blue colour used in Scotch eggs.

E132 Indigo carmine ▲▼★●

Blue colour used in meat products and gravy mixes.

E133 Brilliant blue ▲

Blue colour used in bacon-flavoured snacks and canned peas.

E142 Green S ▲

Green colour used in canned peas, asparagus soup, mint sauce, lime drinks and jellies.

E150 Caramel ▲

Brown colour produced from sugar and used in drinks, gravy mixes, soups, sauces, breads, cakes, biscuits, vinegar, marmalade and beef products.

E151 Black PN ▲

Black colour used in fruit sauces.

E153 Carbon black or vegetable carbon ▲●

Black colour from burnt vegetable matter used in fruit juices, jams and jellies.

E154 Brown FK ▲●

Brown colour used in kippers and other smoked fish.

155 Chocolate brown HT ▲▼★●

Brown colour used in a wide range of processed foods.

E200 Sorbic acid ●

Preservative to slow growth of yeasts and moulds. Used in yogurt, cheese products, wrapped cakes, cake fillings and toppings, sweet sauces, soft drinks and frozen pizzas.

E210 Benzoic acid ▲▼●

Preservative that occurs naturally in tea and raspberries, but is made synthetically for use in fruit products, pickles, marinated fish and salad dressings.

E211 Sodium benzoate ▲▼●

Preservative used in bottled sauces, soft drinks, sweets and prawns.

E212 Potassium benzoate, E213 Calcium benzoate, E214–219 Hydroxy-benzoate salts ▲★●

Same uses as for E210.

E223 Sodium metabisulphite ▲

Preservative used in sausages, bottled sauces, pickled onions, packet mashed potato and orange cordial.

The symbols indicate which groups of people may have reactions to each of the additives listed:

▲ hyperactive

▼ asthmatic

★ aspirin-sensitive

● people with other allergies and intolerances

■ babies

E249 Potassium nitrite, E250 Sodium nitrite ▲●■

Preservatives used in sausages, cooked and cured meat.

E251 Sodium nitrate ▲●■

Used in the same way as E249, and also in some cheeses.

E252 Potassium nitrate ▲●■

Used for curing and preserving meat.

E270 Lactic acid ■

Preservative used in margarines, baby milks, salad dressings, confectionery and soft drinks.

E310 Propyl gallate, E311 Octyl gallate, E312 Dodecyl gallate ▲▼●■

Antioxidants added to fats and oils, so found in fried foods and snacks.

E320 Butylated hydroxyanisole (BHA) ▲▼●■

Antioxidant used in raisins, potato snacks, biscuits, pastry, sweets, breakfast cereals, bottled sauces, ice creams, margarines, soft drinks and prepared fried foods.

E321 Butylated hydroxytoluene (BHT) ▲▼★●■

Antioxidant similar in use to E320.

E406 Agar ●

Thickener and stabilizer extracted from seaweeds and used in ice creams, frozen trifles and meat glazes.

E407 Carrageenan (Irish moss) ●

Emulsifier, thickener and gelling agent extracted from seaweed and used in ice creams, jellies, frozen trifles, spray creams, cake decorations and cheeses.

E413 Tragacanth ●

Emulsifier, thickener and stabilizer extracted from the gum of certain *Astralagus* trees. Used in processed cheeses, cake decorations, sherbet and salad dressings.

E414 Gum arabic ●

Thickener, emulsifier and stabilizer from the gum of acacia trees. Used in packet cream cheeses and gâteau mixes.

E421 Mannitol (manna sugar) ●

Texture improver and sweetener extracted from seaweed and certain ash trees. Used in sweets and ice creams.

E430 Polyoxyethylene (8) stearate, E430 Polyoxyethylene stearate ●

Emulsifiers and stabilizers used in baked goods.

508 Potassium chloride ●

Salt substitute and gelling agent.

510 Ammonium chloride ●

Used for flavour in yeast goods.

514 Sodium sulphate ●■

Used to dissolve other additives.

541 Sodium aluminium phosphate ●■

Raising agent used in cake mixes.

621 Monosodium glutamate (MSG), 622 Monopotassium glutamate ▲▼★●■

Extracted from sugar beet or seaweed. Used as flavour enhancer in meats, soups, savoury snacks and many pre-packed meals.

623 Calcium glutamate ▲▼★■

Used in the same way as 621.

627 Sodium guanylate, 631 Disodium inosinate, 635 Disodium-5-ribonucleotides ▲★●■

Flavour enhancer used in savoury snacks, packet soups, gravy granules and pre-cooked rice dishes.

924 Potassium bromate ●

Used to bleach white flour, therefore found in bread, cakes, pastries and biscuits.

925 Chlorine ●

Used to bleach white flour, therefore found in bread, cakes, pastries and biscuits.

926 Chlorine dioxide ●

Used in the same way as 925 and to purify water.

Improving your
CHILD'S DIET

Many parents find it difficult to persuade their children to eat more healthily and to stop craving junk foods. This is not surprising in a world where our children are bombarded on a daily basis with advertising campaigns designed to switch them on to processed food and drink loaded with sugar, salt, caffeine, additives and hydrogenated fats. However, the task

Below: Instead of potato chips and salted nuts, give seeds, which are much healthier and just as good to eat.

is not impossible. You have more power in their lives than you may think and by presenting your children with attractive, tasty alternatives you can gently direct them away from the junk food.

On the page opposite there are a few suggestions for nutritional alternatives with which to start stocking your store cupboards and refrigerator.

Ideally, of course, you should help your children to develop a taste for real, wholesome food from the word go, not even letting them get addicted to junk food. As we shall see later, food habits and addictions start to develop as soon as a baby is given solid foods. If you are not careful, by the time they reach the toddler stage they may already be hooked on refined sugar and processed foods.

GETTING CHILDREN INTERESTED

If you were in the position where you had chosen to eat in a restaurant and your meal was simply thrown on your plate rather than arranged, the chances are that you would be far less inclined to eat it. The same goes for children, particularly toddlers, for whom eating is a new and exciting experience. You will stand a far greater chance of getting your child to eat certain foods if they are presented to them in an attractive or fun way.

KISS GOODBYE	SAY HELLO
Fizzy drinks	Fresh fruit drinks and water
Sweets	Dried fruit, nuts and seeds
Chocolate and cocoa	Carob substitutes, stuffed dates
Margarine, lard	Natural, cold-pressed oils, butter
Tea	Herbal infusions with honey
White bread	Wholemeal bread, pitta bread, rye bread
White rice	Brown rice, wild rice, pearl barley, millet, quinoa, whole grains
Sweet biscuits	Oatcakes, rice cakes or wholewheat crackers spread with peanut butter
Salt	Vegetable bouillon powder
Refined sugar	Honey, date sugar, molasses, natural maple syrup
Crisps and salted nuts	Vegetable crudités with dips, unsalted nuts, seeds, baked potato wedges
Cakes	Oatmeal flapjacks, bran muffins
Canned vegetables	Fresh or frozen vegetables
Canned fruit in syrup	Fresh fruit
Fishfingers	Homemade fishcakes, fish fillets, tuna
Burgers, sausages, processed meats	Tofu, nut loaves, chicken breasts and other lean cuts of meat
Sugary cereals	Sugar-free muesli, porridge
Sweet fruit yogurts	Live natural yogurt with fruit purée and honey
White flour	Wholegrain flour, stone-ground flour, rice flour, millet flour
Ice cream and ice lollies	Naturally sweetened non-dairy sorbets and ice creams and frozen fruit-juice lollies

Above: Your child is far more likely to be persuaded to eat certain foods if they are presented in an attractive or fun way. Food that is colourful and easy to pick up is particularly appealing.

TODDLERS

The worst thing you can do with a food-fussy toddler is to force them to eat food they do not want. Children will eat when they are hungry, and if you make a big deal out of mealtimes, they will use the food issue as a way of wielding power over you. Dr Christopher Green, author of *Toddler Taming*, suggests that the toddler should sit and eat with the rest of the family, as kids learn primarily from imitation. However, if you have a large household and mealtimes tend to be noisy, busy affairs, it may be better to feed the little one first. This will allow you to sit quietly with your child and encourage them to enjoy the food.

Do not worry if your child does not eat every morsel. But at the same time make sure they eat the healthy, nutritious bits first. If a child knows that there is an exciting pudding coming, they learn very quickly to leave the more 'boring healthy stuff'.

Snacking can be a good way for a toddler to fill up on nutritious food. Slices of fruit, crudités, raisins, bananas, cheese cubes, mini bagels, muffins, rice cakes, oatcakes and flapjacks are all perfect food f or a busy toddler on the go.

TODDLER TIPS

★ Make the food as colourful as possible. Fresh fruit and vegetables are bursting with colour. Put together platters of vegetable sticks, grapes, apple slices and cubes of cheese. Next to this, a pale processed meat sandwich on white refined bread, with maybe a few crisps on the side will suddenly look dead in comparison.

★ Keep food bite-sized and easy to pick up and hold.

★ Let toddlers play with their food. This is normal and part of the learning experience.

★ Change the eating venue from time to time. Have a picnic in the garden, or even inside if the weather lets you down.

★ Play 'hunt the snack'. Hide healthy goodies around the house and help your toddler to find them. They will be quick to eat things up if it means they can do it again.

★ Make the food into shapes and faces. You may not be Picasso, but your child doesn't know that.

★ Divide wholemeal sandwiches into a jigsaw and get toddlers to put the pieces back together. Not only do they eat, but they get to learn as well.

★ Get toddlers to create their own food pictures. Spread a piece of wholemeal toast with peanut butter or some cheese spread. Give them a selection of chopped-up fruit, vegetables, raisins and seeds, and then just let their imaginations run riot. At the end they can eat their masterpiece.

CHILDREN OVER FOUR YEARS

You can talk to older children about the nutritional value of food, and help them to learn as they go along about the difference between healthy food and junk food. Small boys, for example, seem to be very receptive to the suggestion that food will make them strong. If children can identify certain foods as ones that will give them good eyesight, help them sleep, build up their brainpower and so on, they do seem to be more keen to eat them.

Again, presentation can be key to tempting a child's tricky taste buds. Try putting chunky vegetable soup in a hollowed-out crusty wholemeal roll, putting fresh fruit and yogurt in unusual-shaped glasses, presenting fruit and nuts in an upturned paper party hat – use your imagination.

You may also find it helps to take your children food shopping with you. Let them help find the food labels with no hidden nasties, choose the nicest fruit and vegetables. You can play the nutrient game – get them to pick out three foods that contain vitamin C, calcium and so on.

Most children love to help in the kitchen. Even when they are little they can stir the cake mix, knead the dough, pull the grapes off the stalk, wash the salad, even help to weigh the ingredients. As they get older they can then move on to the chopping and peeling stages, operate the blender and juicer, and eventually take their turn at the stove. There is nothing like putting your first meal on the table, and feeling that it was all your own work.

Above: Stimulate your child's interest in a healthy diet by involving him in preparing meals from an early age.

From time to time you can be more adventurous. Get your children to look through recipes and magazines and point out new foods they might like to try. I love watching children from other cultures wading into things that the average western child would turn up their nose at. For example, my Lebanese neighbour's child was addicted to black olives and adored liver. I suppose it is about what you grow up surrounded with, and there will always be a few things each of us dislikes instinctively. I think children are very reluctant to try new things if they believe they are going to have to swallow them. Give them a paper napkin and let them know that it is okay to spit food out discreetly if they dislike it. This may not be great table manners, but it will broaden their culinary horizons.

TEENAGERS

As soon as your children start to hit their teens, they will present you with a whole stack of new factors to consider with regards to their eating habits. As they go through puberty their bodies will change at an

Right: Appeal to teenagers' vanity by emphasizing the positive effect of eating well on their appearance.

Far right: In order to build up a healthy appetite, children should be encouraged to do exercise.

accelerated rate, and so will their mood swings. They will have to deal with increased pressure at school, with things like exams, and the traumas that go hand in hand with becoming aware of the opposite sex.

Growing, active boys will be ravenous most of the time and fixated on building muscle, and girls can all of a sudden start obsessing about their weight and shape. Both will suffer huge anxieties about their skin as the inevitable teenage eruptions commence.

This is a time when their immune and hormonal systems will need as much boosting as they can get, and if you want to sail through this potentially difficult phase of your children's lives, then a nutrient-rich healthy diet will help tremendously.

★ **They** will never have time to eat properly, will drink copious amounts of coffee and diet drinks and will have a nasty habit of turning up with a whole gang of hungry friends when you least expect it.

★ **You** will have to ensure they eat a healthy breakfast before they run out of the door, pray that they eat something with more nutritional value than a chocolate bar at lunchtime, and have a nutrient-packed supper for them in the evening.

The best way to get teenagers to eat healthily is to play up the muscle-building, skin-enhancing, hair-glossing and nail-strengthening qualities of foods. Appealing to their vanity rather than their common sense does tend to do the trick.

A healthy diet can go a long way towards keeping a teenager as mood-, spot- and lethargy-free as

possible, but certain nutrients should be focused on as they are vital for this period in their development.

Iron: This is very important during puberty, especially for girls who are just starting to menstruate. It prevents anaemia and helps build up the immune system. It is found in green leafy vegetables, dried fruit, poultry, red meat, red lentils and wholegrain rice.

Magnesium: Teenagers often suffer from low magnesium levels. This can worsen pre-menstrual stress and increase the severity of allergic reactions. It is needed to ensure the thymus gland functions correctly and is vital for production of antibodies. Good sources are egg yolks, dried fruit, whole grains, green leafy vegetables, nuts and seeds.

Vitamin E: A powerful antioxidant, this vitamin is vital for boosting resistance to infection. It also has the added bonus of being excellent for the skin. Increase intake of avocados, nuts, seeds, vegetable oils, wheatgerm and oatmeal.

Zinc: Zinc is key to maturation of sex hormones, so is essential during puberty. It is depleted in the body by excessive consumption of coffee and caffeine-rich soft drinks. It is also needed for the production of white blood cells. Good sources are poultry, game, red meat, nuts, seeds, shellfish, prawns, oily fish, wheatgerm and whole grains.

EXERCISE

There are no two ways about it, you are going to stand a much better chance of your children wolfing down your lovingly prepared, nutritious fare if they are

ravenous. Playing videos, net surfing and watching the television do not exactly build up an appetite. They may send your children into a zombie-like stupor that needs to be rectified with a quick fix of junk, but we are not talking real hunger here, just plain boredom.

Children need to stimulate their metabolic rates and burn off calories, and the best way to do that is to exercise. Try walking to school with your children if it is practical and enrol them in extracurricular sports clubs, such as basketball, volleyball or swimming. Maybe even invest in a bike for yourself and accompany them to the local park from time to time. They will be far more amenable if there is a fun element to exercise, and particularly keen if it means that Mum or Dad is getting involved, too.

ALWAYS TRY TO BE A GOOD ROLE MODEL

Of course, all these pages of good advice and helpful facts are practically worthless if you do not practise what you preach. Good nutrition is caught, not taught. Children are natural mimics and the chances are that if you eat a diet based on junk and unhealthy food, so will they. Even if you have only just woken up to the fact that a nutritious diet is fundamental to maintaining good health and high energy levels, it is never too late to begin. And the earlier you ensure that your children are eating food that is nourishing, rather than depleting their bodies, the better. Remember, they are counting on you.

THE GOOD DRINK/BAD DRINK GUIDE

Drinking sufficient fluids throughout the day is vital for active children. Depending on their age and the weather, they need between ½ and 1½ litres (1–2½ pints) of liquid per day.

But what liquid?

Water is the best option every time, and you should encourage your children to drink water at mealtimes and throughout the day. If they think water is too boring, dilute it with fruit juice.

What fruit juice?

Commercially prepared fruit juices and cordials quite often contain high levels of additives and sugar, so opt for one that is as natural as possible. The best way is to make your own juice – freshly made juice contains the maximum levels of vitamins, minerals and phytonutrients. Invest in a juicer and start off on simple combinations such as carrot and apple or orange, pear and kiwi fruit. Then, if your children develop a taste for fresh juice, you can begin to incorporate more unusual fruits and vegetables into their diet. Even raw beet-root is sweet and fantastic when combined with oranges and carrot.

Herbal teas such as blackcurrant and camomile are also great and can be drunk hot or chilled over ice.

Are there any drinks children should avoid?

Drinks that are high in caffeine, such as coffee and many soft drinks, actually dehydrate the body, so they have a counter-productive effect. They also inhibit the absorption of calcium, so they are not a great option for your children.

The importance of three
SQUARE MEALS

Kids may eat vast amounts at one meal and pick at the next. They may eat like there is no tomorrow one day and, when tomorrow comes, eat next to nothing at all. There is no need to worry. If they have been encouraged to remain in touch with their body's cues to hunger and satiety, children will eat the amount they need – growth and activity will dictate most of that. So don't fret too much about portion size. Concentrate on ensuring that the three meals you give them are healthy and nutritious, and that there are sufficient healthy snacks available to keep them going when the going gets tough.

THE BIG BREAKFAST

Most pre-packaged children's cereals – almost all sugar and no nutrition – are as bad as no breakfast at all. They can leave your child sluggish and lacking in energy. In order to give them a good start to the day, it is imperative to provide a decent breakfast, or you run the risk of 'morning dopiness'. If they do not start the day with sufficient fuel in their systems, they will usually be hungry by mid-morning, and this will affect their performance. According to American nutritionist Demory Luce, 'breakfast eaters have a better overall diet, have less trouble concentrating and fewer behavioural problems in school', and 'breakfast should be a priority'.

Above: A healthy breakfast is a priority. Give muesli sweetened with honey rather than sugar-coated cereals.

An ideal breakfast includes some protein, a little fat, plenty of carbohydrates and a good source of calcium. Healthy options include:

★ Porridge loaded with wheatgerm, honey and plenty of fresh fruit.
★ Scrambled eggs on wholemeal toast with a glass of fresh juice.
★ Sugar-free muesli with dried fruit, seeds and nuts, moistened with apple juice and live natural yogurt, or soya milk.

Left: A packed lunch of fruit, carrot sticks, a tuna salad sandwich and homemade biscuits is guaranteed to help a school child through the mid-afternoon energy slump.

★ A peanut butter sandwich and glass of calcium-fortified orange juice.

If you use commercial cereals, then opt for sugar-free, wholegrain varieties such as shredded wheat or natural puffed rice. It is also a good idea to vary the type of milk that children put on their cereal. Experiment with goats', soya or rice milk. This is vital if your child has a lactose intolerance. Many leading nutritionists recommend that children avoid a diet high in dairy products, because they are mucus-forming. If you are giving your child cows' milk then it is better to opt for semi-skimmed rather than full fat, unless your child's diet is particularly low in fat.

ACTION-PACKED LUNCHES

Many schools, especially primary schools, do not provide cooked school dinners. This means that children have to rely on parents providing them with a healthy, sandwich-based lunch in a box.

A lunch to get kids through a busy afternoon should include a good source of protein, such as low-fat turkey breast, hard-boiled egg, low-fat cheese, tofu or peanut butter. Protein has the effect of not only supporting tissue growth and maintenance, but also helping to keep the child alert. A meal made up of carbohydrates only can induce drowsiness, which

just compounds the effects of naturally lower biorhythms that occur mid-afternoon. The ideal lunch should also contain a source of complex carbohydrates for time-released energy, such as a sandwich made with wholegrain bread, and a source of fat for staying power – try using olive oil to moisten the bread or dress a packed salad. The lunch should also include a pot of calcium-rich yogurt, fortified soya milk or some tahini spread. The fat content of the lunch should not be so low that hunger will set in

LUNCHBOX IDEAS

★ **Bagel with peanut butter, yogurt, apple**
★ **Tuna salad on wholemeal bread, baby carrot sticks, homemade biscuits, glass of soya milk**
★ **Hard-boiled egg, cherry tomatoes, bran muffin, banana**
★ **Tortilla rolled up with low-fat turkey breast, cheese and lettuce, bag of nuts and raisins**
★ **Pasta salad with tuna and sweetcorn, pear**
★ **Wholemeal pitta bread stuffed with falafels, hummus, parsley and grated carrot, small tub of fresh fruit salad**

Left: Where possible, buy hard-shelled nuts such as walnuts and pecans and shell them yourself. They retain more of their vital oils than the pre-shelled variety.

long before dinner, but it should be low enough to be healthy. Although the jury is still out on the optimum fat content for kids' diets, I suggest that you try to aim for a diet that contains 20–25 per cent fat. This means that if your child is consuming 2,000 kilocalories per day, then 400–500 of them should be provided by fat. To give you a rough idea of how to achieve this, 30 g (1½ oz) of brazil nuts, a 30 g (1½ oz) chunk of Cheddar cheese and 60 g (2½ oz) of chicken roasted with the skin together provide around 400 kilocalories.

Children going through a growth spurt will eat a huge amount, but will drop back when the spurt is over. This makes it unnecessary to get caught up in how many calories they need at lunch, because that will vary from day to day. What is important to know is what a good lunch should include. The following list outlines some good items to pack for lunch:

★ A small carton of soya milk or a yogurt.
★ Generous amounts of complex carbohydrates (for example wholemeal bread, bagel, wholewheat crackers, pasta).
★ A moderate serving of high-quality protein (for example tuna salad, low-fat cheese, sliced sandwich meats or peanut butter).
★ A small amount of fat (for example peanut butter, nuts, avocado or homemade healthy treats that contain fat such as a flapjack).
★ A piece of fruit or some fresh vegetable crudités.
★ A small bottle of water or juice – it is very important to avoid dehydration.

Lunch should definitely not include many, if any, sugary foods. When children are short of time, they may go for sugary foods first, leave the nutritious sandwich, and then suffer a major energy let-down a couple of hours later when the sugar boost has worn off. If you do include treats, try to make sure they have some nutritional value, for example homemade fruit and vegetable breads or oatmeal biscuits with raisins.

Be realistic in the size of the lunch you supply; children often do not have much time to eat at school. It is also important to include a mid-morning snack. Small children often cannot go a whole morning without getting hungry.

SERIOUSLY SENSIBLE SNACKS

Some parents believe that snacking is bad for children, but nothing could be further from the truth. About 20 per cent of a child's energy and nutrients can come from snacks.

Snacks should provide the energy that hungry kids need, as well as the nutrients they might have missed at meals. Some children are overwhelmed by huge platefuls of food, so healthy grazing could be just the answer.

Ideal snack fare includes ready-to-eat vegetables and low-fat dips, raisins or other dried or fresh fruit, fig-type or oatmeal biscuits, wholewheat crackers and calcium-rich snacks such as low-fat yogurt, mozzarella 'string' cheese, calcium-fortified juices, and small bags of unroasted nuts and seeds.

Above: Everyone, and growing children in particular, should eat five portions of fruits and vegetables daily.

HIGH FIVE

You should aim to feed your child five servings of fruits and vegetables per day. These should be divided into three portions of vegetables, for example:

★ 50 g (2 oz) chopped vegetables
★ 50 g (2 oz) green leafy vegetables
★ 25 g (1 oz) dried peas or beans

and two portions of fruit, for example:

★ one piece fresh fruit
★ 175 ml (6 fl oz) 100 per cent fruit juice or 15 g (½ oz) dried fruit

This can be easily achieved if your children:

★ Start the morning with a glass of 100 per cent fruit juice.
★ Have a sandwich or pitta bread with salad at lunchtime.
★ Eat a piece of fresh fruit, such as a banana, apple, orange, pear or a handful of grapes, for a morning snack.
★ Munch on carrot and celery sticks as an afternoon snack.
★ Eat a dark green vegetable, such as broccoli or spinach, at dinnertime, and have a little side salad.

DYNAMO DINNERS

In the evening, children should be lured away from the television to enjoy a proper sit-down dinner with their parents, siblings or carer. This is the time to catch up on any missing servings of vegetables and fruits – as well as on the family's news and gossip!

One of the key requirements of dinner is that it should be easy to digest, with a calming effect. If your child is prone to tummy aches and constipation, apply food-combining principles. This tends to make food more easily digestible. The basic rules are:

★ Do not combine carbohydrates and proteins in the same meal as this slows down digestion. Fats are classed as neutral.
★ Do not give fruit as a dessert. It is better to eat fruit as an appetizer 20 minutes before the main meal. This is because fruit is digested far quicker than most other foods, and if taken on top of a heavy meal it can literally ferment, causing gas and bloating.

Some good meal suggestions are:

★ Melon as a starter, grilled chicken with broccoli and cauliflower cheese, baby gem lettuce.
★ An apple as a snack before dinner, baked potato with guacamole and mixed salad.
★ Small bunch of grapes, stir-fried vegetables with tofu and toasted sesame seeds, salad.

Avoid sugary food and fizzy, caffeine-laden drinks in the evening. This will make your children overly active and restless at bedtime.

GOING ORGANIC

Before the Second World War, there was no such thing as chemically dependent farming. In those days everything was grown in compost-fertilized soils, fruits and vegetables were eaten in season, maximizing on freshness, flour was stone-ground and we did not eat foodstuffs full of nutrient-leaching white sugar. The nutritional picture today is very different:

★ Fields are sprayed with herbicides, pesticides and fungicides.

★ Intensive farming methods are stripping the soil of vital minerals.

★ Demand for out-of-season fruits and vegetables mean they are being picked before they ripen, then transported and stored in refrigerated containers. By the time they reach the shelves at the supermarket the nutritional value has already been stripped.

★ Animals for human consumption are injected with antibiotics and hormones.

★ Meat is kept fresh with nitrates and nitrites, which are converted into potential carcinogens by the body.

★ Freezing, preserving, refining and processing destroy many nutrients.

WHAT IS CHEMICAL FARMING DOING FOR US?

★ According to a study by the US Department of Agriculture in 1998, since 1945, the share of crops lost to insects increased by 20 per cent, despite a 3,300 per cent increase in the use of pesticides.

★ Alarmingly, in 1942 only seven species of insects were resistant to pesticides, today there are 504.

★ In the same study, a comparison was made between 38 minerals in organic and conventional apples, pears, corn, potatoes and wheat. The organic foods averaged about twice the nutrient content and contained 29 per cent less lead, 25 per cent less mercury and 40 per cent less aluminium.

WHAT ARE THE IMPLICATIONS FOR YOUR CHILDREN?

The long-term effects of pesticide residues in our food supply are not fully understood. We do know, however, that the risks are real, especially to infants and children. Babies' bodies are more physiologically

By the age of five, many children have ingested up to 35 per cent of their entire lifetime's allowed dose of some carcinogenic pesticides ...

vulnerable to pesticide residues because their organs and reproductive systems are immature and growing rapidly. Children are also at a greater risk from exposure than adults. By the age of five, many children have ingested up to 35 per cent of their entire lifetime's allowed dose of some carcinogenic pesticides, according to the National Campaign for Pesticide Policy Reform in the USA. When you consider facts like these, going organic really does seem the only option. But what exactly is an organic product?

The term 'organic' refers not to specific agricultural products but to how they are produced. Organic production is based on a sustainable system of farming that maintains and replenishes the fertility of the soil. Organic foods are produced without using systemic and persistent chemical pesticides, herbicides and fertilizers. They are minimally processed to maintain the integrity of the food without artificial ingredients, preservatives or irradiation.

HOW EASY IS IT TO OBTAIN ORGANIC PRODUCE?

Most supermarkets have caught on to the increased demand for organic food, and now it is much more widely available than previously. In many areas there are companies offering to deliver a weekly box of

Left: Organic carrots are particularly worth buying, as carrots absorb lots of potentially harmful chemicals from the soil. At the very least, peel or scrub them well.

organic produce straight to your door. You will receive fruits and vegetables that are in season, naturally reared meat and convenience foods that are free from additives.

Although organic foods tend to cost a bit more, with luck this should be balanced out by the lack of expensive sugary snacks and fizzy drinks in your trolley. Prices for organic foods reflect many of the same costs as non-organic foods in terms of growing, harvesting, transportation and storage. Certified organic foods must also meet strict regulations governing all these steps, so the process is often more labour- and management-intensive. In addition, prices also depend on the item, the time of the year, the place of purchase and the retailer's pricing policy.

HOW DO I KNOW THAT A PRODUCT IS ORGANIC?

'Organic' is a term defined by law, and all organic food production and processing are governed by a strict set of guidelines. Producers, manufacturers and processors all pay an annual fee to be registered as 'organic' and they are required to keep detailed records, ensuring a clearly traceable path from farm or production plant to table.

Each European country has its own national organic certification authority, which conforms to EU standards. These have certification bodies, which may apply additional specifications on top of the EU standards. EU standards, in turn, are subject to those laid down by the International Federation of Organic Agricultural Movements (IFOAM).

In the USA, organic standards are laid out by the Department of Agriculture. Independent certification bodies such as the National Organic Program apply much more stringent conditions and states tend to have their own organic programmes, too, although in general they adhere to the IFOAM guidelines.

TEN REASONS TO BUY ORGANIC PRODUCE

1 Protects our children's health
The average child receives four times more exposure than an adult to at least eight widely used cancer-causing pesticides in food. This exposure to harmful residues in food will impact on their lives in the future.

2 Protects the quality of our water
Pesticides contaminate ground water and pollute the primary source of drinking water for many people. Organic growers and processors use practices that eliminate polluting chemicals and nitrogen leaching.

3 Protects and builds our topsoil
Organic farmers consider soil to be their most important resource. Rather than relying on synthetic fertilizers, they build their soil with composted manure, cover cropping and/or diverse crop rotations.

Organic farming may be one of the few ways forward possible for family farms and rural communities.

4 Strict standards assure integrity

Organic certification standards are the public's assurance that their food and products have been grown and handled according to strict sustainable procedures without prohibited inputs.

5 Reduces potential health risks

Many pesticides were registered long before extensive research linked these chemicals to cancer and other diseases. The Environmental Protection Agency (EPA) now considers 60 per cent of all herbicides, 90 per cent of all fungicides and 30 per cent of all insecticides to be potentially cancer-causing.

6 Preserves biodiversity

One of the most pressing environmental concerns facing our food supply is the loss of biodiversity – the loss of varieties or species of plants and animals. Many organic growers are aware of this problem and have been collecting and using heirloom seed

Below: Some companies deliver boxes containing fresh seasonal organic produce direct to your door.

varieties for decades. Most conventional farms grow hybridized vegetables and fruits, bred for uniformity, ease of shipping and cosmetic appearance.

7 Sustains rural communities

Organic farming may be one of the few ways forward possible for family farms and rural communities. Many organic farms are independently owned and operated and most are smaller than 40 hectares (100 acres) in size.

8 Protects the health of farm workers

If a health risk to consumers from the use of pesticides may be a problem, the risks are far greater for field workers. A National Cancer Institute study found that farmers exposed to herbicides had a six-times greater risk than non-farmers of contracting one type of cancer.

9 Represents a true economy

Organically grown products may seem more expensive, but retail prices can be deceptive because conventionally raised and priced agricultural products represent only a fraction of the true cost. Current prices for conventionally grown foods do not reflect the costs of government subsidies to conventional agriculture, the cost of contaminated drinking water, loss of wildlife habitat and soil erosion, or the cost of disposal and clean-up of hazardous wastes generated by the manufacturing of pesticides. Consumers can pay now or pay later.

10 Taste

All you have to do is try an organic tomato to realize just how tasteless our conventionally farmed produce has become.

A *healthy*
BALANCED DIET

For children to grow up healthy and strong, it is important for them to have what is known as 'a balanced diet'. This means a diet that not only contains all the correct nutrients – proteins, carbohydrates, fat, vitamins, minerals and water – but also provides them in the correct proportions.

An easy way to visualize this is to look at the Food Guide Pyramid below. As you can see, the group of foods at the bottom of the pyramid – bread, cereal, rice and pasta – should form the bulk of the diet, whereas the fats, oils and sweets at the tip of the pyramid should be consumed sparingly.

It is easy to use the pyramid to choose a healthy diet that meets your child's particular needs. Let's take a look at each of the recommended food groups.

Below: The Food Guide Pyramid shows how much of each food group your child should be eating every day.

fats, oils and sweets

milk, yogurt and cheese

meat, poultry, fish, beans, eggs and nuts

vegetables

fruits

bread, cereal, rice and pasta

Bread, cereal, rice and pasta –
6–11 servings a day
1 serving = 1 slice of bread, ½ bagel or bun, 1 medium muffin, 25 g (1 oz) dry cereal, 25 g (1 oz) cooked cereal, 25 g (1 oz) cooked rice, 25 g (1 oz) cooked pasta, four small crackers.

Vegetables – 3–5 servings a day
1 serving = 50 g (2 oz) raw leafy greens, 25 g (1 oz) any other chopped vegetable, 175 ml (6 fl oz) vegetable juice.

Fruits – 2–4 servings a day
1 serving = 1 medium apple, banana, orange or similar, 25 g (1 oz) chopped fruit or berries, 175 ml (6 fl oz) fruit juice.

Milk, yogurt and cheese –
2–4 servings a day
1 serving = 250 ml (8 fl oz) milk or yogurt, 40 g (1½ oz) natural cheese, 50 g (2 oz) processed cheese, 100 g (3½ oz) cottage cheese.

Meat, poultry, fish, beans, eggs and nuts – 2–3 servings a day
1 serving = 50–75 g (2–3 oz) of cooked lean meat, poultry or fish, 1 egg, 50 g (2 oz) cooked beans, 2 tablespoons peanut butter, nuts or seeds.

Above: Aim to serve your children 60–75 per cent of their food raw and uncooked. Fresh salads are perfect.

Fats, oils and sweets

Use sparingly. Focus on heart-healthy unsaturated fats, such as those found in vegetable oils, nuts, seeds and avocados and minimize sweet intake.

OPTING FOR RAW FOOD

Most nutritionists recommend that the bulk of our diet should be made up of raw, unadulterated food. You should really be aiming to ensure that 60–75 per cent of your children's diet is raw and uncooked. There are several reasons for this. First and foremost, heat produces a marked change in the composition of food. It totally destroys the vital life-enhancing enzymes and causes losses in vitamin and mineral content of anything between 5 and 100 per cent, particularly when food is cooked in water. Heat causes coagulation of proteins, making them more indigestible. It also changes the composition of fats and can cause the production of carcinogenic substances if fat is overheated. Raw food moves far quicker through the colon, preventing constipation and toxic build-up.

There are plenty of ways in which you can make raw food easy and fun to eat. Here are some ideas:

★ Make fresh fruit juices and smoothies; these are vitamin- and mineral-packed tonics in a glass.

SOME SAMPLE DIETS

Sample diets for kids at three calorie levels:

Toddlers and children up to the age of about 6

To provide 1,600 calories:

Bread group servings	6
Vegetable group servings	3
Fruit group servings	2
Milk group servings	2–3
Meat group	150 g (5 oz)
Total fat	50 g (2 oz)
Total added sugars *	25 g (1 oz)

Children aged 6–10 years and teenage girls

To provide 2,200 calories:

Bread group servings	9
Vegetable group servings	4
Fruit group servings	3
Milk group servings	2–3
Meat group	175 g (6 oz)
Total fat	75 g (3 oz)
Total added sugars	50 g (2 oz)

Teenage boys

To provide 2,800 calories:

Bread group servings	11
Vegetable group servings	5
Fruit group servings	4
Milk group servings	2–3
Meat group	200 g (7 oz)
Total fat	100 g (3½ oz)
Total added sugars	75 g (3 oz)

★ Include a salad with one meal a day. Find the salad vegetables your little ones like most and always have a bowl to hand at mealtimes.

★ Use plenty of crudités and dips made with raw ingredients such as avocados, nuts, bananas, yogurt and seeds.

★ Add grated or chopped vegetables to rice and noodle dishes at the last moment for extra crunch.

NUTRIENTS

As you well know, your car would underperform, maybe even break down, if you filled it with the wrong fuel, forgot to check the oil levels or let the water run dry. The human body works on the same principle. It has certain basic nutritional requirements that need to be fulfilled in order for it to function properly.

So what exactly does it need to remain healthy? Basically, the body requires all six major nutrients: protein, carbohydrates, fat, vitamins, minerals and water. All are equal in terms of importance. Each has specific functions and they are all interrelated either directly or indirectly. Not one of them can work without the assistance of one or more of the others.

PROTEINS

After water, the most abundant substance in the body is protein. This is because not only the muscles, tissues and skin but also the hormones, enzymes, antibodies and blood are made of protein. Even after the intensive growth years of childhood, proteins play a vital role in maintaining and rebuilding our bodies as they cope with the wear and tear of daily life.

Proteins are made up of different combinations of 24 amino acids. All but nine of these amino acids can be produced in the human body, and the ones that cannot be made are known as essential amino acids. They have to be supplied in the diet. The

Above: Fish is an excellent form of protein, which is absolutely vital for growing children.

essential amino acids are methionine, threonine, leucine, isoleucine, lysine, tryptophan, valine, phenylalanine and histidine.

For the body to utilize protein effectively, all of the essential amino acids have to be present. If they are not, then a protein deficiency will result and this can have serious implications for growing children.

When a food contains all the essential amino acids, it is termed a 'complete protein'. Most of the complete protein foods come from the animal kingdom: eggs, meat, dairy products and fish. There are some plant foods that are complete proteins, for example soya beans, nuts, seeds, whole grains, legumes, wheatgerm, pollen, spirulina and brewer's yeast, but the majority of plant foods are incomplete proteins. These have to be combined to create complete protein meals. The best way to achieve a complete protein meal without animal products is

Left: Grains such as brown rice are important sources of carbohydrate, which provides the energy needed for all bodily functions.

to have grains and legumes together; for example beans and rice, whole wheat with tofu, barley and lentils, and so on.

If you are following a vegetarian diet, it is usually best to include some animal protein such as cheese, eggs or milk, or take supplements such as spirulina, brewer's yeast or wheatgerm to achieve a complete protein intake. It is also possible to obtain specific amino acids from health food shops that can be taken in the form of tablets.

CARBOHYDRATES

Carbohydrates provide the energy necessary for all bodily functions, especially those of the brain and central nervous system. They also help in the digestion and assimilation of foods, as the body needs carbohydrates to metabolize proteins and fats.

Protein will act as a secondary source of energy and heat when there is a shortage of carbohydrates and fat. But this is not ideal, because when the body starts to burn off its own valuable protein for energy, a deficiency results. This is why it is so important for a balanced diet to always include the body's primary source of energy: carbohydrates.

With the exception of milk, carbohydrates come exclusively from plant sources: fruits, vegetables, grains, legumes, honey and sugar.

All sugars and starches are carbohydrates, and they break down into three categories:

★ Simple sugars or monosaccharides: glucose (blood sugar) and fructose (fruit sugar).
★ Double sugars or disaccharides: lactose (milk sugar).
★ Complex carbohydrates or polysaccharides: starches and cellulose (potatoes, rice, grains and dietary fibre).

Our bodies can use only the simple sugar called glucose to provide energy; everything else – sugars, starches, and to a lesser degree proteins and fats – has to be converted into glucose by digestive enzymes before it can be utilized by the body as energy. The more complex the structure, the longer it takes. Any excess is converted into glycogen and stored in the liver and the muscles, or under the skin as fat reserves.

Certain carbohydrate foods, such as biscuits, sweets and cakes made from refined sugar or refined flour, lack essential vitamins, minerals and fibre. These are known as empty calories and can promote obesity. Natural sources of carbohydrates should be encouraged. For example, an orange has the same number of calories as a tablespoon of refined sugar, but it also contains valuable nutrients and fibre.

35

FATS

Fats, or lipids, are the most concentrated form of energy and contain the highest calorific value per gram. For this reason, many adults try to cut fats from their diets altogether, and then use the same principle for their children's diet. But growing children need a certain amount of fat. We all do. It is just that adults get into the 'calorie trap' and do not appreciate that the energy requirements of active children are much higher than those of more sedentary adults.

Fat is a very necessary part of the human body for a number of reasons:

★ It stimulates gall bladder activity.
★ It helps absorb vitamins A, D, E and K as well as calcium.
★ It is needed to form hormones.
★ It is vital for maintaining glossy hair and soft skin.
★ It keeps us warm, provides energy and protects our vital organs.
★ It is essential for brain development and function.

Not all fats are created equal. The key is to provide a diet that contains the correct amount of the right sorts of fat. But which fats are healthiest? There are two types – saturated and unsaturated. Unsaturated fats are usually liquid at room temperature and include vegetable and fish oils. Saturated fats are solid at room temperature and usually come from animals, for example lard and butter. Coconut oil and palm oil are the only vegetable sources of saturated

fats. Our bodies can process unsaturated fats into heat or energy far more easily than saturated fats, which tend to be stored as fat around the body.

Fats are broken down into fatty acids and glycerol by the digestive process. These fatty acids give fats their different texture, flavour and melting point. All the fatty acids can be manufactured by the body, with the exception of three: linoleic acid, linolenic acid and arachidonic acid. These are known as essential fatty acids and have to be supplied by the food we eat. The two main families of essential fatty acids are omega-3 and omega-6. Omega-3 fatty acids keep the skin and other tissues youthful by preventing dryness and scaliness. Darker-fleshed oily fish are a good source. Omega-6 fatty acids are necessary for the transport and breakdown of cholesterol and are found in oils such as soya bean, corn and safflower. It is important to take both types in combination. Canola oil has a good balance of both.

In general, vegetable oils are the best source of essential fatty acids, but the more processed they are, the lower the essential fatty acid content. So it is always better to opt for unrefined and cold-pressed oils. Do not be duped into thinking that margarine is good for your children; it is usually so highly processed it contains even less fatty acids than butter. A word on labelling to look out for and avoid is 'hydrogenated' – this means that the vegetable oils have been converted into fat at an extremely high temperature, turning it into an unhealthy option.

A diet that lacks the essential fatty acids can lead to eczema, psoriasis, fatigue, scaly skin, dry hair and even obesity. But beware, overconsumption of even unsaturated fats can lead to oxidation in the body, which will increase the formation of free radicals. This can contribute to premature ageing, heart attacks and cancer. You may think this is hardly the concern of a child, but bear in mind that you are in the process of creating your children's taste in food and eating habits for the rest of their lives, and good habits learned early on will improve their chances of good health in later years.

DIETARY FIBRE

Cellulose or dietary fibre is a polysaccharide and belongs to the carbohydrate family. It can be found only in natural carbohydrates in the skins and walls of fruits and vegetables and in whole grains. Even though it is essentially non-nutritive, it plays a major role in the body, where its main job is keeping the colon running efficiently. It does this by exercising the intestinal muscles, which encourages regular elimination. If the diet is lacking in fibre then it could result in constipation, haemorrhoids, appendicitis, diverticulosis or even diabetes.

WATER

The human body is made up of approximately 70 per cent water, so this has to be classified as a major nutrient. Your child should be drinking at least six glasses of water or fruit juice mixed with water per day. This is particularly important if the diet is lacking in fresh fruits and vegetables, which are made up primarily of water. Encourage your child to drink more water by offering it more often. First thing in the morning, at mealtimes, after exercise and play, by their bed at night – water needs to be around all the time, as it is so easy to forget to drink.

VITAMINS

Vitamins are found in small and varying quantities in all natural animal and vegetable foods. There are about 20 different vitamins that play a vital role in human nutrition. They interrelate with each other to support and maintain all bodily functions. If food is the body's fuel, then vitamins could be classed as the spark plugs. They do not contain calories, but contribute to our overall health by stimulating metabolic processes, converting food into energy, helping to create blood, skin and bone, detoxifying the body and enabling reproduction to take place.

Below: Bulgar wheat is a good source of dietary fibre which, although not nutritionally important, keeps the colon running efficiently.

Right: Like other orange fruits, papaya is a good source of vitamin A, which benefits eyesight and helps the body combat colds and infections.

Most vitamins are water-soluble and are measured in milligrams (mg). Any excess in the body is eliminated with urination. Some are fat-soluble and measured in International Units (IU). These can be accumulated in the body, and prolonged overdosing can have a detrimental effect.

Vitamin requirements vary tremendously from person to person, depending on gender, age, life-style and metabolic rate. Nutritional needs may increase dramatically during illness, stress, crisis and convalescence. Certain allergic conditions can also necessitate a higher dosage of certain vitamins. The best way to achieve optimum health is to provide a balanced diet with an abundance of natural nutrients.

Vitamin A
Fat-soluble. Occurs in two forms in nature: retinol and carotene. Retinol is found in animal foods such as fish oils and liver. It is stored in the liver and is readily used by the body if there is adequate protein intake. Carotene is abundant in root vegetables, leafy greens and yellow fruits. It cannot be used by the body until it has been converted into retinol, a process that requires fats and bile.
Beneficial effects: Fights colds and infections, maintains mucous membranes and helps them resist infection by bacteria. Helps eyesight, as it is necessary in formation of the photosensitive pigment visual purple. This is vital for night vision. It helps to maintain a healthy skin and prevents kidney stones.
Deficiency symptoms: Red itchy eyes, night blindness, dry or rough skin, broken tooth enamel, kidney stones, colds and infections, allergies.

Best natural sources: Fish liver oil and animal liver, eggs, carrots, yams, sweet potatoes, pumpkin, yellow vegetables, yellow fruits such as apricots, peaches, papaya, cantaloupe melon, milk and dairy products.

Vitamin B complex
All of the B complex vitamins are water-soluble. They are vital for the conversion of carbohydrates to glucose and food to energy. If they are not present in the diet then carbohydrates do not 'burn' fully, leading to fatigue, constipation and indigestion.
Top tip: The water-soluble B vitamins readily dissolve in water, so when cooking vegetables or brown rice, retain the water for use in sauces or soups as it is a concentrated source of natural vitamin B complex.

Vitamin B1 (thiamine)
Thiamine is important for converting carbohydrates into glucose. It is quickly absorbed by the body, but cannot be stored, so daily intake is vital. White sugar, white flour, caffeine and antibiotics can block its absorption.
Beneficial effects: Known as the 'morale' vitamin, it has a positive effect on the central nervous system, so can be vital during times of stress. It can alleviate a poor memory, relieve depression and stabilize appetite and stomach secretions. It is important for growth and can calm motion sickness.
Deficiency symptoms: Nervous disorders, low thyroid function, appetite loss and heart palpitations.
Best natural sources: Brewer's yeast, rice bran, raw wheatgerm, whole grains, peanuts, green and yellow vegetables, fruit, milk.

38

Left: Raw wheatgerm contains several of the B vitamins, which are so important for the conversion of food into usable energy.

Vitamin B2 (riboflavin)

Vitamin B2 cannot be stored in the body. It can withstand heat, but not light. The vitamin functions as part of an enzyme system that breaks down carbohydrates, fats and proteins.

Top tip: Do not keep milk in clear containers, as the light will destroy the riboflavin content.

Beneficial effects: Contributes to good vision and maintains healthy skin, hair and nails. Promotes growth and the assimilation of iron, helps to convert tryptophan (amino acid) into niacin (vitamin B3), can help bring relief to eczema sufferers and counteracts a sweet tooth.

Deficiency symptoms: Mouth and lip lesions, red itchy eyes, tongue inflammations, scaly skin, anaemia and dental problems.

Best natural sources: Milk, liver, brewer's yeast, dairy products, leafy green vegetables, fish and eggs.

Vitamin B3 (niacin and niacinamide)

Niacin can be found in plants, and is formed in the body from the essential amino acid tryptophan, when sufficient B2, B6 and protein are present in the diet. It can be stored in small amounts in the liver. Deficiencies occur when taking antibiotics or indulging in too many sweets.

Beneficial effects: Assists macro-nutrient metabolism, strengthens digestive and nervous systems, improves blood circulation.

Deficiency symptoms: Bad breath, headaches, indigestion and fatigue.

Best natural sources: Liver, brewer's yeast, raw wheatgerm, fish, eggs, peanut butter, dried fruits, avocados.

Vitamin B5 (pantothenic acid)

Although present in most foods, many people do not get enough vitamin B5. A deficiency reduces blood sugar levels, which results in exhaustion. Pantothenic acid is necessary for macro-nutrient metabolism, and the synthesis of fats, cholesterol and antibodies.

Beneficial effects: Stimulates adrenal function, prevents fatigue, increases antibody production and helps fight infections. It also reduces the toxic effect of antibiotics.

Deficiency symptoms: Mental stress, allergies, hypoglycaemia, indigestion, constipation, ulcers, fatigue, skin disorders.

Best natural sources: Royal jelly, cod's roe, meat, raw wheatgerm, liver, kidneys, whole grains, beans, brewer's yeast, molasses, nuts.

Vitamin B6 (pyridoxine)

Vitamin B6 is vital for the release of glycogen from the liver when the muscles need energy. It assists with the metabolism of protein and balances sodium and potassium in the body, therefore regulating body fluids, acid–alkaline balance and the function of the nerves and muscles. It is partially destroyed by cooking and removed totally from grains by refining.

Beneficial effects: Inhibits the release of histamine, so can be of benefit to allergy sufferers. Also prevents anaemia and controls oily skin and dandruff.

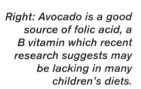

Right: Avocado is a good source of folic acid, a B vitamin which recent research suggests may be lacking in many children's diets.

Deficiency symptoms: Skin striations, linear nail ridges, photosensitivity, cracks around the lips, convulsions in children, hypoglycaemia, diabetes, appetite loss, allergies, anaemia, water retention.
Best natural sources: Brewer's yeast, liver, kidney, raw wheatgerm, molasses, cabbage, milk, eggs.

Vitamin B12 (cyanocobalamin)

Although vitamin B12 requirements are tiny and are measured in micrograms (mcg), it is one of the most important of the B group. It hardly ever occurs in non-animal foods, so vegetarians should ensure that they take pollen, spirulina or brewer's yeast to counteract this, particularly if they do not eat dairy products. Vitamin B12 is essential for the functioning of all the cells in the body, from the bone marrow to the nerves.
Beneficial effects: Together with folic acid, B12 forms red blood cells in the bone marrow, promotes growth and appetite in children, increases energy, improves brain functions such as memory, learning ability and balance, maintains the nervous system, and helps the action of iron, vitamin C, pantothenic acid, folic acid and choline.
Deficiency symptoms: Most severe is anaemia. Sore tongue, fatigue, apathy, loss of coordination, impaired memory and lack of concentration.
Best natural sources: Liver, kidneys, meat, eggs, dairy produce, spirulina.

Vitamin B15 (pangamic acid) Works

with vitamins C and E as a powerful antioxidant.

Beneficial effects: Eliminates environmental toxins from the body, extends cell lifespan and increases general immunity.
Deficiency symptoms: Fatigue, glandular and nervous disorders.
Best natural sources: Brewer's yeast, brown rice, whole grains, pumpkin, sesame seeds.

Folic acid This important vitamin works with

B12 in the synthesis of nucleic acids and certain amino acids. It is easily destroyed by antibiotics, and supplementing the diet with large doses of vitamin C can deplete folic acid, so its consumption should be raised accordingly. This is one of the vitamins that recent research revealed to be lacking in many children's diets.
Beneficial effects: Stimulates stomach secretions, which help to guard against food poisoning and improve digestion. Also stimulates formation of red blood cells with B12, promotes mental and emotional health and raises blood histamine levels.
Deficiency symptoms: Anaemia, lack of appetite, digestive disturbances, poor growth, lesions at the corners of the mouth,
Best natural sources: Green leafy vegetables, liver, egg yolks, torula yeast, carrots, cantaloupe melon, pumpkin, avocado, beans.

Vitamin C (ascorbic acid) A powerful

water-soluble vitamin that is highly unstable and easily lost in cooking, and even when fruit and vegetables are peeled or soaked. It is also easily perishable in

the human body, so we require a daily intake that should be spread throughout the day for maximum benefit.

Beneficial effects: Vitamin C improves our ability to absorb calcium, iron and certain amino acids. It also enables the body to excrete poisonous substances such as copper, lead and mercury. It increases our immune response by boosting antibody function and has powerful antihistamine properties that alleviate allergies. It helps to prevent anaemia (with B12 and folic acid), and speeds up the healing processes of the body when it is wounded. In addition, it is also a powerful antioxidant.

Deficiency symptoms: Regular colds, infections and allergies, anaemia, bleeding gums, fatigue, broken capillaries and poor healing of wounds.

Best natural sources: Whole citrus fruits and juices, peppers, broccoli, tomatoes, cabbage, green leafy vegetables, melons, yams, potatoes.

Vitamin D

Known as the 'sunshine vitamin', vitamin D is fat-soluble and is supplied by either food or exposure to the sun, which converts cholesterol under the skin into vitamin D. After absorption it is stored in the liver, and in minute quantities in the brain, skin and bones. Vegans and people who do not drink milk should supplement their diet with vitamin D, which increases the excretion of magnesium from the body, so a magnesium supplement should be taken to counterbalance this.

Beneficial effects: Aids absorption of calcium and phosphorus, therefore essential for infants and children whose bones are developing. It helps the body to assimilate vitamin A and maintains a healthy nervous system.

Deficiency symptoms: Soft and porous bones and teeth, tooth decay, fatigue, short-sightedness.

Best natural sources: Fish liver oil, sardines, herring, salmon, tuna, fortified milk.

Vitamin E

Fat-soluble, this vitamin is a powerful antioxidant. It plays a key role in pituitary hormone production, which among other things controls childhood growth.

Beneficial effects: Antioxidant, assists cellular regeneration, guards against the effects of pollutants in food, water and air, accelerates healing and inhibits the actions of carcinogens.

Deficiency symptoms: Poor growth and healing of wounds and burns, fatigue, circulatory disorders.

Best natural sources: Vegetable oils, raw wheatgerm and wheatgerm oil, soya beans, leafy green vegetables, whole grains and cereals, eggs.

Vitamin K

Fat-soluble vitamin synthesized by the intestinal flora. In order to absorb vitamin K, there must be an adequate consumption of cultured milk products and vegetable oils.

Beneficial effects: Aids the liver in production of prothrombin (necessary for blood clotting).

Deficiency symptoms: Metabolic defects, a malfunctioning liver, colitis or coeliac disease will cause a vitamin K deficiency. A sure sign is poor

Right: Sunflower seeds contain calcium, the most abundant mineral in the body and vital for building and maintaining bones and teeth.

blood clotting and regular nose bleeds. All the fat-soluble vitamins must be emphasized in the diet, along with calcium and B complex.

Best natural sources: Alfalfa, kelp, green leafy vegetables, yogurt, buttermilk, egg yolks, fish liver oil, safflower and soya bean oil.

MINERALS

Calcium Calcium is the most abundant mineral in the body. It needs vitamins A, D and C, phosphorus, magnesium and protein for proper absorption.

Beneficial effects: Builds and maintains bones and teeth, maintains healthy nervous system and muscle function, can help insomnia if taken at bedtime, helps blood clotting and promotes a healthy complexion.

Deficiency symptoms: Porous and brittle bones, fractures, tooth decay, rickets, muscle aches, cold sores and mouth blisters, impaired growth.

Best natural sources: Milk and dairy products, sesame seeds, sunflower seeds, peanuts, walnuts, soya beans, green vegetables.

Phosphorus This mineral works hand in hand with calcium and is present in every cell. It is vital for the release of energy in the body and for the conversion of glucose to glycogen.

Beneficial effects: Maintains healthy bones and teeth, promotes growth and body repair, provides energy by metabolizing carbohydrates, maintains the acid–alkaline balance in the blood and tissues.

Deficiency symptoms: Weak bones and teeth, rickets, gum infections, loss of appetite, muscle weakness.

Best natural sources: Meat, eggs, fish, whole grains, raw wheatgerm, nuts and seeds.

Potassium Potassium is mainly found in the intracellular fluids of the body. It regulates the sodium–potassium balance in the body, stimulates kidney function, maintains a proper acid–alkaline balance and is essential for muscle contraction.

Beneficial effects: Helps the body dispose of waste products, increases the supply of oxygen to the brain, lowers blood pressure, stimulates insulin secretion and prevents over acidity.

Deficiency symptoms: Fluid retention, irregular heartbeat, nervousness and fatigue.

Best natural sources: Citrus fruits, tomatoes, green leafy vegetables, bananas, whole grains, potatoes and pineapple.

Sodium Most sodium is found in the extra-cellular fluids of the body. It works in conjunction with potassium to regulate acid–alkaline balance in the blood. It enables oxygen and digested nutrients to flow in and out of the cells, and helps with transmission of nerve impulses.

Beneficial effects: Stimulates the kidneys and keeps minerals soluble, stimulates the secretion of gastric juices and promotes sweating.

Deficiency symptoms: Intestinal gas, weight loss, muscle wasting, fatigue, dehydration.

Best natural sources: Salt, shellfish, kelp, meat, celery, beetroot, carrots, asparagus, dandelion greens, watermelon.

Magnesium

Magnesium is mostly to be found in the bones, but a smaller part is found in the tissues and blood, where it activates metabolic enzymes. The mineral helps the body utilize vitamins C and E and helps convert glucose to energy. It can be depleted by a diet that is high in refined flour and sugar.

Beneficial effects: Maintains strong bones and tooth enamel, gives healthy muscle tone, acts as a natural tranquillizer and improves urine retention, so helpful for bed wetters.

Deficiency symptoms: Weak muscles, jumpy nerves, bed wetting, irregular heartbeat.

Best natural sources: Figs, lemons, grapefruit, yellow corn, nuts, apples, raw wheatgerm, green vegetables.

Sulphur

Vital for glossy hair, healthy skin and strong nails. It is important for the formation of collagen.

Beneficial effects: Improves mental abilities, maintains healthy skin, hair and nails and treats psoriasis, eczema and dermatitis when it is used in ointment form.

Deficiency symptoms: Rough skin, dry hair, brittle nails, arthritis.

Best natural sources: Eggs, radishes, onions, celery, string beans, kale.

TRACE ELEMENTS

Iron

Iron is the most abundant metallic trace element in the body. It is vital for the formation of haemoglobin, which carries oxygen from the lungs to every cell in the body.

Beneficial effects: Relieves fatigue, prevents anaemia, promotes the immune system, aids growth.

Deficiency symptoms: Anaemia, pallor, shortness of breath, brittle nails.

Best natural sources: Liver, kidneys, oatmeal, dried peaches, raisins, prunes, egg yolks, molasses, dried beans, spinach, sesame seeds.

Zinc

Zinc is essential for growth and development, and maintaining the immune system's ability to fight infectious diseases and diarrhoea.

Beneficial effects: Lowers histamine production – good for allergies – speeds up healing of wounds, stimulates growth, helps to form insulin, increases natural immunity.

Deficiency symptoms: Retarded growth, poor wound healing, fatigue, susceptibility to infections, lack of appetite, allergies, white spots on nails.

Best natural sources: Meat, fish, raw wheatgerm, mushrooms, kelp, brewer's yeast, pumpkin seeds, egg yolks, dried legumes, almonds, milk, alfalfa.

Copper

Copper helps the body absorb iron and aids the development of bones, nerves and connective tissue. It also converts the amino acid tyrosine into a dark skin pigment for skin and hair.

43

Right: Dried beans are a good source of iron.

Far right: Mangetout meanwhile are a good source of copper, which helps the body to absorb iron.

Excessive copper can be damaging, so if your water supply comes from copper taps, let the water run for a couple of minutes before using it.

Beneficial effects: Helps iron form haemoglobin and prevent anaemia, lowers histamine effect, helps the body utilize vitamin C.

Deficiency symptoms: Anaemia, fatigue, skin depigmentation.

Best natural sources: Soya beans, legumes, whole wheat, prunes, liver, seafood, green vegetables, molasses.

Manganese

Manganese takes part in the synthesis of cholesterol and fatty acids, helps to metabolize carbohydrates, to form thyroxin, the major hormone of the thyroid gland, and to produce the neurotransmitter choline. If there is a high intake of calcium and phosphorus, this will increase the need for manganese.

Beneficial effects: Helps to prevent diabetes, guard against muscle–nerve disorders, promotes muscle strength and improve brain function.

Deficiency symptoms: Skeletal abnormalities, low tolerance of carbohydrates, loss of muscle condition.

Best natural sources: Nuts, whole grains, green leafy vegetables, peas, cloves, ginger.

Chromium

Chromium is removed from common foods by refining, but it is essential for the metabolism of glucose, so plays a vital role in energy levels.

Beneficial effects: Helps to metabolize sugar, regulates blood sugar level, prevents onset of diabetes and hypoglycaemia.

Deficiency symptoms: There is debate as to whether these exist, but many nutritionists associate fatigue, slow growth, obesity and impaired glucose metabolism with a chromium deficiency and claim to get good results if chromium levels are raised.

Best natural sources: Brewer's yeast, molasses, raw wheatgerm, rice bran, meat, shellfish.

Iodine

Iodine is concentrated in the thyroid gland and helps to make up the hormone thyroxine. It raises the metabolic rate and helps the body burn fat. It also regulates the rate at which the body cells use oxygen, so promoting growth and energy, and improving mental functions.

Beneficial effects: Reduces body fat, calms nervousness, increases energy, promotes healthy skin and hair, guards against tooth cavities, increases resistance to colds.

Deficiency symptoms: Obesity, dry hair, rapid pulse, cold body, constipation, low resistance to colds and infections, nervousness, weakness.

Best natural sources: Kelp, seaweeds, shellfish, onions, garlic, pineapples, citrus fruits.

Selenium

Selenium works best with vitamin E, and is a powerful antioxidant. It plays a vital role in bolstering the immune system.

Beneficial effects: Increases immunity to disease, promotes energy, anti-ageing.

Deficiency symptoms: Fatigue, susceptibility to infection.
Best natural sources: Raw wheatgerm, tuna, onions, nuts, seeds, brewer's yeast.

Fluorine Fluorine is essential for the formation of strong bones and teeth, but overdosing of the mineral can be toxic.
Beneficial effects: Promotes formation of strong bones and teeth, prevents tooth decay.
Deficiency symptoms: Poor tooth development in children, tooth decay.
Best natural sources: Kelp and seafoods, carrots, fluoridated drinking water, garlic, sunflower seeds, almonds.

PHYTONUTRIENTS

Phytonutrients are powerful antioxidants that work hand in hand with vitamins and minerals to keep degenerative disease at bay and maintain a healthy immune system. Only recently discovered, there are thought to be over a hundred different types.

The simplest way to ensure you are preparing food rich in these compounds is to include naturally colourful fruits, vegetables and even seaweed in your child's diet.

★ **Lycopene** is found in red food, primarily tomatoes.
★ **Curcumin** is present in yellow food such as corn and yellow peppers.

DOES MY CHILD NEED SUPPLEMENTS?

As much as possible, nutrients should come through diet. Taking large doses of dietary supplements cannot substitute for eating wisely, and will not teach a child to make appropriate food choices. Also, excessive doses, especially of fat-soluble vitamins such as vitamins A and D, can actually cause harm.

★ The nutrients that are most likely to be deficient in a child's diet are calcium, iron, zinc, vitamin C, vitamin A, folic acid and vitamin B6. In particular, children who consume little or no dairy products are at particular risk of calcium deficiency, which can interfere with bone growth and development.
★ If you suspect that your children are lacking a certain vitamin or mineral, it would be wise to check first with a nutritionist before putting them on a course of supplements. Nutritional needs vary from person to person and it is important to choose the correct combination for each individual.

★ Yellow **anthoxanthins** are abundant in potatoes and yellow-skinned onions.
★ Fruits or vegetables with a good orange colour are rich in **carotenoids**. These benefit the immune system in particular. Eat plenty of cantaloupe melon, mangoes, carrots, apricots and squash.
★ **Anthocyanidins** and **proanthocyanidins** come in purple or blue fruit. Raise your intake of berries, black cherries, black grapes and blackcurrants.
★ **Chlorophyll** promotes quick healing and guards against diseases such as cancer. Wherever you see green, you'll find it. Include some of these every day: cabbage, broccoli, kale, salad leaves, seaweed, wheatgrass, algae such as spirulina.

45

Feeding & weaning
BABIES & TODDLERS

Below: Breast milk contains all the antibodies and nutrients babies need, in a readily absorbable form.

Goats' milk is better than cows' milk for weaning babies as its composition is far nearer to that of breast milk.

NIPPLE OR NOZZLE?

If you want to boost your baby's immune system, protect against allergies and prevent infections, then there really is nothing better for your baby than breast milk. Human breast milk is full of antibodies, antioxidants, minerals such as zinc, selenium and iron, enzymes, essential fatty acids and antimicrobial factors, all of which are far more readily absorbed than the nutrients in commercial milk formulas and pasteurized cows' milk.

The breast milk produced in the first three days, colostrum, is full of white blood cells, which increase the baby's immunity to disease. It also begins the infant's bowel movements by introducing a high level of bacteria into the gut. Breast-fed babies are less prone to constipation than their bottle-fed counterparts.

Breast milk is made up of much finer globules than cows' milk and contains ten times more vitamin E and more lactose, which helps the baby maintain healthy intestinal flora and aids brain development. It also contains less protein and smaller quantities of minerals. This difference in protein levels is no accident. Think of the size of a calf and compare that with a human baby; no wonder that research suggests that babies weaned on cows' milk are more prone to obesity in later life.

Above: Your baby's first solid foods should be home-made, using fresh vegetables, fruit and whole grains.

If breast-feeding is not an option for you, then there are a couple of factors you should consider to improve the quality of the formula milk you use:

★ Formula milk does not contain as many essential fatty acids as breast milk. These are necessary to regulate the immune system. Nutritional expert Lucy Burney suggests adding a few drops of flaxseed oil into bottled milk to provide omega-3 fatty acids. Do not go over 1 teaspoon per day.
★ Breast milk contains beneficial natural bacteria called bifidus. It is possible to get hold of products containing bifidus that can be added to formula milk. Ask your chemist or health food store for more details.

FIRST SOLIDS

At four to six months of age most babies show signs of being ready to start the transition to solid foods. However, there are no hard and fast rules about this and starting babies on solids before they are physically ready may cause choking. Several signs will indicate that a baby is ready to try out solids:

★ The birth weight has doubled.
★ Good control of head and neck has developed and the baby can sit up with some support.

LOOKING AFTER YOURSELF

When you are breast-feeding it is vital that you provide yourself with a balanced diet. Your baby is relying on you to provide all the nutrients necessary for normal growth and development and if you want to breast-feed your baby for the optimum period of nine to 12 months, then you really do have to take your health very seriously. Your little one will be taking the best from you, and if you let yourself become depleted of biochemical reserves such as calcium and phosphorous, it can have long-term effects on your health.

★ Eat plenty of fresh fruits and vegetables. Dark green vegetables, such as spinach, are a fantastic source of extra calcium and iron. Calcium is very important at this stage, because if there are not sufficient quantities in the diet for the baby, then it will be drawn from the mother's bones.
★ Avoid junk food laden with empty calories, and snack on healthy alternatives such as seeds and nuts.
★ Try to achieve a balanced diet full of all the major nutrients, and eat regularly.
★ Super-boost your system with plenty of vitamin- and enzyme-packed fresh juices.
★ Remember to drink plenty of water.
★ Replace caffeine-laden drinks such as tea, coffee and fizzy drinks with herbal teas.
★ If you do feel your diet is lacking, consider taking supplements such as essential fatty acids and keep your immune system strong with plenty of vitamins A, C and E, and selenium.
★ Keep your diet based on natural whole foods, and eat lots of raw food.
★ Do not smoke, as this depletes vitamin C reserves, and avoid alcohol as this has a detrimental effect on most nutrients, particularly the B group vitamins.

COOKING TIMES FOR WHOLE GRAINS

★ Rice – simmer for 30–40 minutes, purée or mash.
★ Millet – simmer for 5–10 minutes, purée or mash.
★ Quinoa – simmer for 25–30 minutes, purée or mash.

★ The baby can show fullness by turning the head away or by not opening the mouth.
★ The baby begins showing interest in food when others are eating.

As a general rule you should always try to give your child fresh, homemade food where possible. Commercially prepared baby foods are often high in sugar, salt and water, which can start off some early addictions. Sugar also upsets the metabolism of calcium and can lead to glandular imbalance and an impaired immune system.

The three key foods for babies at this stage are fruits, vegetables and whole grains. To start with it is best to keep to single ingredient purées and to introduce your baby to one at a time. This way you can watch for any food intolerances. The consistency should be quite runny, as this will help your baby make the transition to solid foods more easily. Try adding a little goats' milk or apple juice if the purées seem too thick. Begin with 1–2 tablespoons of solid food a couple of times a day and gradually build up to 3–4 tablespoons. Do not add flavourings to your baby's food; get them used to clean, natural tastes from the very beginning. And never add salt or any other condiments.

Fruits

Fresh, uncooked fruits such as apricots, avocados, melons, kiwi fruits, mangos, papayas, peaches, plums and bananas should be chopped finely and mashed or puréed. Apples and pears should be steamed until soft, then mashed or puréed. Avoid citrus fruits and strawberries.

Dried fruits, such as figs, prunes and raisins, are fine. Soak the fruit for about 12 hours, then purée or mash them.

Vegetables

Vegetables such as beetroot, broccoli, carrots, green cabbage, kale, parsnips, pumpkins, spinach, swedes and sweet potatoes should be steamed and mashed or puréed. Make a simple vegetable stock from any combination of the above and add to the purées if they are too thick.

Avoid potatoes, tomatoes, peppers and aubergines before your baby is nine months old, as these can cause a reaction.

Whole grains

Rice, millet and quinoa are good grains to start with, as they are gluten-free. They can be ground into a flour-like consistency in a grinder and cooked with a little filtered water, breast or formula milk to make highly nutritious porridges. They can also be mixed with fruit purées and a little molasses to create different tastes.

SIX TO EIGHT MONTHS

At six months your baby will probably still be taking breast or formula milk three to five times per day. Gradually, however, this will begin to level off as solid foods become a source of nutrition.

Above: From about six months, most babies show an interest in feeding themselves. Encourage them with finger foods.

At this stage, expect your baby to consume solids four times per day. The portions should be about 2–3 tablespoons. This is obviously dependent on the size of the child and how well the child eats. Gradually increase the consistency of the food.

Ring the changes with your baby's drinks. Try fruit juices diluted with filtered water, mix goats' milk with carrot juice, and don't forget good old filtered water.

★ If you are buying fruit juices, ensure they do not contain added sugar. Ideal ones to try are apple, grape or orange.

★ Delay introducing orange juice until your baby is nine months of age if your family has a history of allergy to orange juice.

★ Do not give juices in a bottle at bedtime as this may lead to tooth decay.

Try to balance your baby's intake of fruit and vegetables. Some dieticians recommend introducing a few vegetables before fruits as the sweetness of fruit may make a less-sweet food such as vegetables less appealing.

As soon as babies start to show an interest in feeding themselves, try offering finger foods in small amounts. Avoid any foods that could cause choking, such as apple chunks or slices, grapes, sausages, popcorn, nuts, seeds and hard chunks of uncooked vegetables. Instead, soft-cooked vegetables (for example carrots or green beans) or washed and peeled soft fruits (for example slices of banana or peaches) are good finger foods. Teething foods, such as strips of toast, unsalted crackers, bagels and teething biscuits may also be introduced.

EIGHT TO 12 MONTHS

Breast or formula milk should still be offered three to four times per day at this age. At eight to 12 months of age, you can expand your baby's repertoire of foods. Try introducing organic poultry, game and meat purées, pulse and bean purées and fish purées. Simmer any of the above in natural vegetable stock until fully cooked and soft, then purée or mash.

The introduction of iron-rich foods, such as green leafy vegetables or a little blackstrap molasses, is important at this stage as breast milk is not a rich source of iron, but infants have adequate iron stores to last until eight months of age.

As with other foods, offer one new type of meat, fish or pulses at a time, in 3–4-tablespoon servings, and make sure that it is all finely ground. Serving sizes for fruits and vegetables also increase to 3–4 tablespoons, four times per day. Egg may be given three or four times per week, but only the yolk until the baby is one year old, as some babies are sensitive to egg whites.

49

Above: Healthy snacks like carrot sticks are ideal for toddlers, who often prefer to eat little and often.

It is also time to start getting a little more adventurous with your combinations of fruits and vegetables. Try any of the following: avocado and apple, butternut squash and spinach, sweet potato and parsley, broccoli and parsnip, carrot and swede, apple and mango, melon and kiwi fruit, banana and papaya, Jerusalem artichoke and celeriac. The list is endless. Imagine how healthy your baby will be on such a healthy, vitamin-packed diet.

By the age of 12 months, most children are off the bottle. From now on, if your child still uses a bottle, it should contain water only.

ONE TO FOUR YEARS

When a child reaches the age of one year, whole milk may replace breast milk or formula milk. Goats' milk is a good choice, and if your child shows signs of lactose intolerance experiment with soya milk as a substitute. Children under the age of two years should not be given low-fat milk as they need the additional calories from fat to ensure proper growth and development.

Children under the age of one should not be given any dairy products, but now you can start to introduce cheese, cottage cheese and yogurt in small amounts. Even though cows', goats' and soya milk are not as nutrient-dense as breast or formula milk, the one-year-old child should be achieving a balanced supply of nutrients from meats, fruits and vegetables, breads and grains, and dairy products.

Providing a variety of foods will help to ensure adequate intake of vitamins and minerals. Toddlers do not grow as rapidly as babies do, so their nutritional needs relative to their size decrease during the second year of life (although they continue to gain weight, they no longer 'double their weight' as infants do). Keep in mind, however, that toddlers become more and more active as they learn to crawl and walk. Toddlers and small children will usually eat only small amounts at one time, but will eat frequently (four to six times) throughout the day.

Below: It makes sense to prepare purée for your baby in bulk and freeze the extra in ice cube trays.

SAFETY PRECAUTIONS

★ If using commercially prepared baby food, feed the baby directly from the jar only if you use the entire jar contents, otherwise use a dish to prevent contamination.

★ Opened containers of food for your baby should be covered and stored in a refrigerator for no longer than two days.

★ Never reheat food.

★ Use a small plastic baby spoon to feed the baby.

★ Avoid foods that may cause the baby to choke (popcorn, nuts, potato chips, whole-kernel corn, berries, grapes, hot dogs, raw vegetables, raisins, dry-flake cereals).

PREPARATION AND STORAGE OF BABY FOOD

Preparing fresh food every mealtime is not really an option. Life can get very hectic when you have a baby and you will often be tired. It is best to make food in bulk and freeze it in ice cube trays.

★ Once you have made your purée, sterilize the ice cube trays by immersing them in boiling water.

★ Pour the purée into the compartments, which usually hold around a tablespoon each.

★ Allow to cool thoroughly before freezing. Once frozen, the cubes can be popped out of the tray and kept in resealable freezer bags, ready for use.

Remove however many you need and allow them to defrost at room temperature. Always let them thaw completely before gently heating.

A couple of important points to remember:

★ Never reheat food more than once.

★ Date all bags, and never give your baby out-of-date frozen food.

As a rough guide, frozen fruit, vegetable and meat purées will last up to three months; frozen fish and pulse purées should be eaten within two months.

Left: Check the labels of commercial baby food and avoid any that contain wheat – gluten can cause coeliac disease if given before your baby is six months old – sugar, additives and salt.

51

Shopping &
PREPARING

Supermarkets are catching on fast to today's consumer demand for healthier alternatives, such as organic fruit and vegetables and whole foods. However, when it comes to specialist foods and supplements, your local health food store may be a better option. If you are changing your whole way of eating, there will be some ingredients that have probably not graced your cupboards before. You may need advice on the choices available and this is more likely to be found in a local health food store than in a supermarket.

FOOD PREPARATION

If you are really going to get into a new, healthier lifestyle for you and your kids, it is essential that you are enthusiastic about it. Many people associate cookery with drudgery, and when you are short of time, the thought of preparing food can be a nightmare – far easier to open a packet straight out of the freezer and shove it in the microwave.

Changing your attitude and actually learning to enjoy food preparation is an essential first step. But there is no need for alarm. The beauty of a lot of healthy food is that it is quick and easy to prepare. You do not have to be a slave to the kitchen.

A well-equipped kitchen can save you time and energy, and is not necessarily expensive. If you

INGREDIENTS TO LOOK OUT FOR IN HEALTH FOOD STORES

★ **Unprocessed cereal grains and related products: wholegrain breakfast cereals, breads and flours.**
★ **Dried beans and pulses.**
★ **Raw seeds and nuts: sunflower, pumpkin and sesame seeds, walnuts, cashews and almonds.**
★ **Special diet foods: low sodium, sugar-free and gluten-free.**
★ **Foods to satisfy a sweet tooth: honey, molasses, maple syrup, dried fruits, fruit concentrates and carob products.**
★ **Herbs, herbal teas and coffee substitutes made from cereal grains.**
★ **Vitamins and mineral supplements.**
★ **Organic produce.**
★ **Specialist supplements such as spirulina, raw wheatgerm, lecithin, brewer's yeast and kelp.**
★ **Soya beans, tofu, soya milk and miso (soya bean paste).**

Right: Fresh juices are one of the best ways of ensuring your children gain the maximum benefit from fresh ingredients.

Below: Health food stores are a good place to look for healthy alternatives to junk food.

cannot afford some of the gadgets below, see page 54 for some alternative budget suggestions.

Food processor: A great invention, particularly if you have to grate and slice large amounts of vegetables, or want to prepare baby food in bulk. They usually come with blender and grinder attachments, which saves on buying them separately.

Blender or liquidizer: These are invaluable if you do not have a food processor. They are great for baby foods, soups, smoothies and sauces.

Grinder: Use to grind seeds and spices, and reduce cereal flakes to a flour-like consistency.

Steamer: The best way to cook vegetables and hard fruits with a minimal loss of nutrients. You can buy a stainless-steel version that fits inside a saucepan, or the more natural bamboo type from an oriental store.

Juicer: There is nothing like a quick hit of fresh juice when you need a boost. They are great for preparing super-charged juice tonics for your children and making fruit ice creams and nut butters. The really good ones are expensive, but the quality of the juice is much better than cheaper versions. Invest in a juicer that pulverizes or masticates the ingredients, the ones that work with a centrifugal action create a lot of heat, which can destroy essential nutrients.

Ice cube trays and freezer bags: These are great for freezing baby purées, meat and vegetable stock and fresh juice cubes for smoothies.

Above: Griddling meat, fish and vegetables instead of frying them cuts down on the amount of oil needed.

HEALTHY COOKING METHODS

Grilling or griddling: Great for vegetables such as aubergines and courgettes, meat and fish. You can get away with using only a very small amount of oil.

Steaming: Unless you are cooking baby food, do not let your vegetables go soft. Too many people reduce vegetables to no more than cellulose skeletons with little nutritional value. Using a steamer and making sure your veggies still have that crispy texture is a far healthier way of cooking. Steamers are also brilliant for cooking fish.

Stir-frying: Finely chopped colourful vegetables and lean strips of meat need only a short time to be transformed into a tasty stir-fry dish. Use the minimum amount of oil, and throw in your favourite fresh ingredients. Add sesame oil, a splash of soy sauce, some beansprouts and cooked rice noodles at the end of cooking. Even the most anti-veggie child should dig in.

Baking: Take one ovenware dish, add a mixture of vegetables, meat or fish together with a drizzle of olive oil and a generous quantity of fresh, chopped herbs, cover and bake. The flavours will infuse and you will have a one-stop meal that is not loaded with unnecessary fat, takes no time to prepare and leaves you free to help with the children's homework.

HEALTH DOES NOT HAVE TO COST A FORTUNE

There are many ways of providing your family with a healthy diet that does not have to break the bank:

★ If you do find organic fruits and vegetables too expensive to buy, be very vigilant about washing and peeling the non-organic variety.

★ You can get amazing bargains if you have a market near you. Turn up at the end of the day to see what is available. Also remember that buying fruit and vegetables when they are in season is always cheaper.

★ If you do find a glut of cheap, seasonal fruit, then it can be frozen either puréed or, in the case of berries, whole.

★ Why not shop with another cost-conscious parent? You can quite often buy in bulk and save a fortune. This may make buying items like organic meat and fish a more realistic proposition.

★ Be more adventurous with grains like pearl barley and rice. Combine with a few beans and legumes, add a few vegetables and you have the basis of a healthy meal, which is still high in protein but a cheaper option than meat.

★ Do not waste your leftovers. Meat and vegetables can be made into wholesome soups. All you need is a blender and some vegetable stock.

★ If you have not got a steamer, no problem. Put a sieve or colander on top of a saucepan of boiling water and cover with the lid. Alternatively, put vegetables or fish in the centre of a piece of greaseproof paper, bring up the edges and make into a closed bag. Secure tightly with string, and place in a pan of boiling water. The beauty of this technique is that you can cook several things simultaneously without the flavours interfering with each other. You can also pop the parcels into the oven in a baking tray with a little water in the bottom. The effect is the same, and children love unwrapping their tasty little parcels.

★ Do not take your children out when they are hungry, particularly to entertainment parks,

Above: Shop for seasonal fruits and vegetables at local markets. Late in the day there may be good bargains.

cinemas or concerts, where the junk vendors will be out in force. If anything, allow them one treat, ideally something like popcorn, and go armed with bags of healthy snacks.

TIME SAVERS

★ **Opt for recipes that can be frozen and make double the quantity.**

★ **Try to buy all dried and non-perishable food once a month, and either get your fresh produce delivered or make just one trip to the shops a week.**

★ **A tip for grains or dried legumes is to put them in a wide-mouthed vacuum flask, cover with boiling water and leave overnight. Think of the energy savings.**

Foods that
ENERGIZE

Are your children always full of vitality with seemingly unlimited energy, or are they often sluggish and lethargic from the moment they wake up? Do they go into overdrive after consuming a sugary snack or soft drink, only to complain of being tired a short while later? Our bodies all need fuel to keep them going, and if your children are exhibiting signs of low energy, then the chances are you are not keeping them topped up with the right sort of fuel.

As we mentioned earlier, carbohydrates are our primary source of energy. They are commonly found in fruits and vegetables, grains and legumes, sugar and honey. As far as children's energy needs are concerned, the general rule is to allow your child 1,000 kilocalories per day, plus 100 kilocalories for every year of age (or allow 20 kilocalories per 500 g /1 lb of body weight). But if your child is highly active, then you can expect those figures to rise, possibly even double.

Sugar is the most abundant source of carbohydrates, but don't kid yourself that I am talking about white, refined table sugar, because I am not. Our bodies can use only the simple blood sugar called glucose to provide energy. Everything else – sugars, starches, and to a lesser degree proteins and fats – has to be converted into glucose by our systems' digestive enzymes before it can be utilized by the body as energy.

MAINTAINING BLOOD SUGAR LEVELS

In order to sustain a feeling of well-being and to have sufficient energy, we need to keep a constant blood sugar level. The body monitors this using a hormonal

Below: Children need a constant supply of fuel from the right sorts of food to give them the energy they need.

56

As far as children's energy needs are concerned, the general rule is to allow 1,000 kilocalories per day, plus 100 kilocalories for every year of age (or allow 20 kilocalories per 500 g/1 lb of body weight).

Right: Store-bought fruit juices may contain extra sugar and other undesirable additives. Make your own whenever possible.

balancing system involving the pituitary gland, adrenal glands, liver and pancreas. The pituitary gland is the brain's main hormonal control centre. It receives messages from gluco-receptor cells in the brain, which keep it updated on the blood sugar situation and then sends on this information via hormones to the adrenal glands, liver and pancreas.

If the blood sugar level rises too high, then the pancreas – the blood sugar regulator – is signalled to secrete insulin. This then converts any excess glucose into glycogen, which is stored in the liver and muscles for future use. On the other hand, if the blood sugar level falls too low, the pancreas is stimulated to secrete glucagon and the adrenal glands to secrete adrenaline, which converts the glycogen back into glucose.

Imagine the constant hammering the poor old pancreas gets when your children keep consuming snacks loaded with refined sugar, which rapidly raises the blood sugar level and then causes it to drop even lower than before. These children are on an energy 'yo-yo' cycle, which causes irritability, low energy, fatigue and lack of concentration.

On a more dangerous level, if the pancreas gets exhausted and insulin production is diminished, then the end result could be diabetes. Or it could become overly sensitized and produce too much insulin, lowering blood sugar and causing hypoglycaemia.

BEWARE HIDDEN SUGAR

The human body, it would seem, has no physiological requirement for refined sugar, so why do parents in the western world keep letting their children consume so much of it?

One reason could be that people are often totally unaware of the number of hidden sources of sugar in processed foods. Look out for sugar that lurks in the everyday foods you would least expect to find it in. Fruit yogurts – often considered healthy options – are often full of sugar, as are some fruit juices, tomato ketchup and canned vegetables. In addition, check the labels of so-called health cereal bars, as these, too, can be a sugar minefield. Remember that even though natural sweeteners such as honey and molasses are better than refined sugar, you can still have too much of a good thing.

If you want your child to be full of energy, to perform well at school and to stand a good chance of not developing conditions such as diabetes, obesity, hypoglycaemia and atherosclerosis, then the answer is clear. Avoid processed food that is laden with sugar and switch to natural alternatives. Your child's diet should include a high level of complex carbohydrates, but this should always be balanced with fibre, protein and a little fat, in order to maintain the delicate balance of blood sugar levels.

57

Above: Dried fruit is a great energy-boosting food as the body can convert it into a readily usable form with ease.

ENERGY BOOSTERS

Simple and double sugars are the most concentrated sources of energy and dried fruits are the best natural energy boosters. They are high in fructose, which is readily converted into glucose by the liver and immediately absorbed from the intestines into the bloodstream, without the need for insulin. This makes dried fruit one of the best 'quick hit' energy-boosting foods available.

The speed with which foods release their sugars varies according to the food. This is measured using the 'glycaemic value'. The higher the value, the quicker the release. For a consistent energy output and stable blood sugar level throughout the day, stick to the slow to moderate sugar releasers. It is a good idea to balance the quick releasers with a small amount of protein, such as tofu, chicken, nuts, legumes, eggs, fish or beans, as this will slow down the digestion and create a more consistent blood sugar level. The addition of fibre also slows down sugar release and should help to guarantee that your child has enough energy to last the day.

★ **Quick sugar releasers:** honey, cornflakes, baked potatoes, all dried fruit, freshly squeezed fruit and vegetable juice, cooked root vegetables.
★ **Moderate sugar releasers:** pasta, brown rice, bagels, corn chips.

★ **Slow sugar releasers:** rye bread, natural yogurt, raw root vegetables, pears, apples, whole grains, legumes.

DRINKS THAT ENERGIZE

If you want to lift the energy levels of a flagging child, the quickest and most healthy step is to juice a pile of fruit and vegetables. Many children and adults reach for a caffeine kick in the form of a cup of coffee or a carbonated drink when their energy levels ebb, but the boost that you get from a fresh juice cocktail is hard to beat, and far better for the body.

Try blending fruit and vegetable juices together, such as carrot and apple, as too many juices made of fruit alone can have a similar effect on blood sugar levels as eating sugar, even though the effect is not quite as drastic. Also, it is best not to have juices on an empty stomach. So when your children's feet start to drag, a handful of nuts and a healthy juice should put them back on track.

If you find that your children tend to run out of energy during the long school day, try supplementing their lunchbox with some of these energy-boosting snacks, which will give them an extra lift:

★ **An apple, a few nuts and some dates**
★ **Flapjacks**
★ **Raw vegetables**
★ **A low-fat yogurt enriched with wheatgerm and a few seeds**
★ **Oatcakes with hummus or an avocado dip**
★ **A chunk of cheese**
★ **Sugar-free cereal bars**

Zippidy Dip
with Crudités

This dip is a child-friendly version of guacamole, minus the chilli and spring onion. It is full of energy-giving nutrients and, if it is served with plenty of fruit and vegetable crudités, a very good source of vitamins and minerals. Avocados are particularly rich in folic acid, vitamin B6 and potassium.

Serves 4

- ● 149 kcals ● 5 g carbohydrate
- ● 2.5 g protein ● 9 g fat ● 3.5 g fibre

2 large avocados
3 tomatoes, skinned, deseeded and chopped
1 garlic clove, crushed
juice of 1 lime or lemon
1 tablespoon chopped coriander leaves
¼ teaspoon ground cumin
¼ teaspoon vegetable bouillon powder
crudités, to serve

1 *Cut the avocados in half and remove the stones. Scoop the flesh into a bowl and mash until smooth. Add the tomatoes, garlic, lime or lemon juice, coriander, cumin and bouillon powder and mix well to make a chunky dip. Alternatively, for a smoother dip, put all the ingredients into a food processor or blender and whiz for 30 seconds.*

2 *Serve the dip with an assortment of crudités such as celery and carrot sticks, apple slices and red pepper strips, or with rice cakes or oatcakes, or spread it on wholemeal toast.*

***For more energizing recipes
see page 94*** ▶▶

A neat idea

For a variation on this dip, mix the avocado with 1 grated apple, the juice of 1 lemon, 50 ml (2 fl oz) apple juice and a handful of toasted sunflower seeds.

Foods for
SPORTS

Exercise is fundamental to your child's normal development. It is needed for growth, to increase muscle tone, to stimulate digestion, for the absorption of nutrients, for the metabolism and for the elimination of waste products. Regular exercise strengthens the blood vessels, lungs and heart and improves the oxygenation of every cell in the body.

THE RIGHT SORT OF FUEL

Children should be encouraged to be active and to spend as much time as possible outside. If children are involved in plenty of physical activity they will burn

Below: Exercise is fundamental to a child's development. It stimulates the absorption of nutrients and aids growth.

a lot of calories and so need extra fuel. Different activities use up different amounts of energy.

The correct diet is vital for an active child to prevent exhaustion and maintain energy levels. When taking part in physical exercise the body will burn a lot of glucose, so there needs to be plenty of stored glycogen in the liver to provide this. The key foods for energy are carbohydrates.

If the diet is lacking in carbohydrates and high in protein, the body will produce ketoses. These toxic compounds need to be eliminated via the kidneys, which can become overworked as they try to rid the body of these potentially dangerous substances.

As already mentioned, there are two basic types of carbohydrates: sugars and starches. Whereas the sugars (monosaccharides and disaccharides) are vital for immediate bursts of energy, the starches (polysaccharides) are better for sustained energy. They take longer to break down, so will keep your

Energy expenditure / hour

Sitting down	80 kilocalories
Standing up	138 kilocalories
Walking	216 kilocalories
Roller-skating	350 kilocalories
Horseriding	480 kilocalories
Running	900 kilocalories

Flapjacks

This is a perfect high-energy snack. The flapjacks are full of complex carbohydrates and rich in natural sugar and iron. They will keep for up to a week if stored in an airtight container. **Makes 12**

- 198 kcals ● 22 g carbohydrate
- 2 g protein ● 11 g fat ● 1.4 g fibre

150 g (5 oz) butter
75 g (3 oz) raw brown cane sugar
75 g (3 oz) blackstrap molasses
250 g (8 oz) porridge oats
25 g (1 oz) dried fruit, such as apricots, prunes or
    sour cherries, chopped

1 *Put the butter, sugar and molasses into a saucepan and heat until the butter has melted – do not let it boil. Mix in the oats and dried fruit and stir thoroughly.*

2 *Press the mixture into a lightly greased 20 cm (8 inch) square tin and smooth the surface with a palette knife. Bake in a preheated oven, 190°C (375°F), Gas Mark 5, for 25–30 minutes, until the flapjack is set and golden brown.*

3 *Mark the flapjack into portions while still warm and leave in the tin for about 5 minutes. Remove them from the tin and leave to cool on a wire rack.*

For more sports recipes see page 98 ▶▶

child going for longer. Key sources of starch to include in the diet are wholemeal breads, pastas and cereals, brown rice, oats, barley, rye, corn, millet, buckwheat, pulses, potatoes and bananas. These foods should make up 50–65 per cent of the diet, along with plenty of fruits and vegetables, protein, fats, fibre and water.

The key vitamin for sports activity is vitamin B12, which can be found in meat, cheese, eggs, fish, milk and milk products. This is vital to increase energy levels and is especially important to watch for in a child who does not eat meat.

Phosphorus is necessary for the metabolism of carbohydrates and is found in all the foods that contain vitamin B12, plus legumes and nuts.

When exercising a lot of fluid is lost through perspiration, so make sure your child drinks up to 3 litres (5 pints) of healthy fluids such as water and juices every day, and has sufficient natural sodium; the best natural source is celery. A great juice to give a child after sports is a combination of fresh celery, cucumber and pineapple. This will calm down a hot child, replenish fluid levels and replace lost sodium.

If your child suffers with cramp after exercise, try including lentils in their diet. It is thought that lentils are good for neutralizing muscle acids.

Remember that junk foods deplete the body of energy, so if your child wants to compete and win, natural wholesome food is the best ally.

Foods that
CALM

Above: Even lively children need to calm down at times. The food they eat can affect how they behave.

Some children are naturally more rambunctious or rebellious than others, and all children go through periods of stress and trauma, whether it involves anxiety about exams, picking up on domestic turmoil within the family or falling out with their friends. Children are also easily excitable: a forthcoming holiday, a birthday party or even a sleepover at a friend's house can be enough to turn some of them into wound-up springs.

For some parents, however, the problem is more serious and calming down their offspring is not easy. More and more children today are prone to

behavioural problems. These children used to be called hyperactive, but are now classed as suffering from 'attention deficit and hyperactivity disorder' (ADHD) or 'attention deficit disorder' (ADD).

ATTENTION DEFICIT DISORDER

According to a recent estimate, 3–4 per cent of American children between the ages of five and 14 are being treated for ADHD or ADD. The number of children under treatment for ADHD nearly tripled between 1990 and 1995. This condition has various symptoms, and hyperactive children usually exhibit many but not necessarily all of the following:

★ **Poor attention:** A poor listener, easily distracted, forgets instructions, visually inattentive, a dreamer, a bad reader.
★ **Impulsive behaviour:** Doesn't think before acting, often branded as aggressive, easily led.
★ **Never satisfied:** Gets stuck on one idea, doesn't learn from experience or know when to stop.
★ **Overactive:** Likes to be on the move, almost motor-driven, fidgety, disruptive.
★ **Variable performance:** Behaviour fluctuates from day to day.
★ **Social handicap:** Trouble mixing with others and

According to a recent estimate, 3–4 per cent of American children between the ages of five and 14 are being treated for attention deficit and hyperactivity disorder.

making friends, speaks without thinking, a poor loser, acts in an extreme fashion to gain attention.

★ **Disorganization:** Confuses left and right, messy eater, untidy, disorderly.

★ **Low self-esteem:** Begins very early and is worsened by lack of social and academic success.

★ **Language problems:** Forgets to complete sentences, interrupts others to avoid forgetting what to say, gets confused about today/tomorrow.

Below: Children with a constant poor attention span who are prone to dreaming and have low self-esteem may be suffering from ADHD.

FOR THE CHILD WITH ADHD

Avoid:
★ **Any foods containing additives**
★ **Fizzy drinks and anything else containing the sweetener aspartame**
★ **Foods with added refined sugar**

Increase:
★ **Organic food where possible**
★ **Rice, lentils and corn**
★ **Whole foods and grains such as brown rice, millet and barley**
★ **Alternatives to cows' milk, such as rice milk, soya milk, nut milks and goats' milk**
★ **Water**
★ **Quality protein, such as poultry, soya, fish, lentils and beans**
★ **Essential fatty acids found in oily fish, seeds and nuts**
★ **Unrefined oils such as sunflower, walnut, olive and sesame**
★ **Magnesium – nature's natural tranquillizer – up that lettuce intake**

★ **Specific learning problems:** Usually has problems in certain subjects.

★ **Sleep problems:** Can't settle, restless.

Recent research has linked ADHD to a problem in brain metabolism. Researchers studied adults who had been hyperactive since childhood and who were parents of hyperactive children. They found reduced activity in those areas of the brain that control attention and movement.

Some parents wonder whether sedentary lifestyles, increased television viewing and larger class sizes might be causing what appears to be an increased prevalence of ADHD. These may or may not be implicated, but to date none of these factors has been seriously studied in relation to ADHD.

But the dietary links cannot be ignored, and this syndrome has been associated with excessive intake of sugar, and the artificial sweeteners, colourings and preservatives found in processed foods and drinks. It is also true that children today are exposed to a range of neurotoxins, such as lead from car fumes and water pipes. Sensitivity to substances such as those in air fresheners, perfumes, toothpaste, bathing products and soaps is also a contributory factor.

It seems clear that many children would be more resilient if they were not so malnourished and lacking in vital nutrients such as zinc, chromium and essential fatty acids, a lack of which has been linked to behavioural problems.

The standard medical treatment for ADHD is stimulant medication, often using a drug called Ritalin® (methylphenidate). For reasons not entirely understood, stimulant medication has a focusing effect on people with ADHD. But with this positive effect come drawbacks. Ritalin, an amphetamine derivative, can cause significant adverse short-term effects in some children, including anxiety, agitation, and tics (up to 3 per cent of patients). It has also

been reported that long-term use of such stimulants could have harmful effects. The efficacy of Ritalin beyond short-term use has not been proven, and the long-term effects of stimulant medication on normal growth and development have not been investigated.

These fears, together with the recent dramatic increase in Ritalin prescriptions, have led a number of parents to seek alternative treatments for this condition. The first port of call is to take a careful look at their child's diet. My niece suffers from the condition and my sister has achieved a high degree of success by modifying her daughter's diet. The key to controlling ADHD with diet is to remove the foods that trigger the behaviour (see box page 63). Keep a check on regularly eaten favourite foods and see if they make symptoms worse.

Preliminary studies on children with ADHD show that calming treatments, such as massage therapy and relaxation training, are useful additions to a careful diet. ADHD is a hard condition to define, it is difficult to treat and can be nearly impossible for adults to endure. There are limitations to all of the treatments discussed here, natural or pharmaceutical. But while none of these treatments is for everyone, the right treatment can lead to dramatic results in the right child.

Below: Whole grains like pearl barley contain the amino acid tryptophan, a natural sleep regulator, which make them ideal ingredients for the evening meal.

Lettuce & Apple
Juice

Lettuce is a natural tranquillizer; it contains small amounts of lactucin, which is known to induce a state of relaxation. The apple, besides being packed full of nutrients, gives this juice a comforting natural sweetness.

Serves 1 (makes 200 ml/7 fl oz)

● 71 kcals ● 14 g carbohydrate
● 1.8 g protein ● 1 g fat ● trace fibre

175 g (6 oz) Romaine lettuce
1 apple, weighing about 250 g (8 oz),
   cut into wedges
ice cubes, to serve (optional)

1 *Put the lettuce and apple into a juicer and juice. Put the ice cubes, if using, into a tall glass and pour over the juice. Serve immediately.*

For more calming recipes see page 102 ▶▶

SLEEP PROBLEMS

Even if your child does not suffer from ADHD, you may have noticed that they become 'hyper' after a 'sugar-free' drink or sweets. This usually indicates that they are having a blood sugar surge after consuming too much sugar, or that the caffeine usually contained in fizzy drinks is stimulating their system to produce too much adrenaline, which will turn them into wound-up springs. This can play havoc with their sleep patterns, particularly if they are eating heavy meals, snacking on junk food or drinking the wrong things late in the evening.

If your child will not calm down in the evening avoid the following at dinnertime:

★ Saturated fatty foods such as red meat, dairy products and hard cheese. These take a long time to digest.
★ Foods containing tyramine, an amino acid found in the nightshade family of vegetables, such as aubergines, courgettes and spinach. It is also found in bacon, ham and sausage. This amino acid stimulates the production of adrenaline.

★ Tea, coffee and fizzy drinks such as cola and chocolate, which all contain caffeine.

But you can increase:

★ Foods rich in calcium and magnesium such as broccoli, cauliflower, mackerel, chicken, salmon, greens and peas.
★ Foods that contain the amino acid tryptophan, a natural sleep regulator. Good sources are whole grains, tuna, bananas, figs, dates and nut butters.
★ Herbal teas and water. You can also replace chocolate with carob, which is caffeine-free.

Foods for
BRAIN POWER

Do you want your children to graduate with first-degree honours? If so then their diet is vital. The brain, like any other part of the body, needs to be well nourished, and if your children are eating unhealthy junk food, the chances are that their brains are being denied the adequate nutrition to function at their best. Amazingly, our brains use 50 per cent of our energy intake, and that level rises when we are involved in lots of mental activity, such as studying for exams.

On the additives front, caffeine and other stimulants deprive the body of vital nutrients, so avoid tea and coffee, chocolate, refined sugar products and caffeine-laden fizzy drinks.

And it is not just food: aluminium is thought to be linked to poor memory, so throw out aluminium pans and do not expose your children to anti-perspirant deodorants, as they contain high levels of aluminium. There is also debate about the effects of mobile phones on the brain. Perhaps it is better to be safe than sorry and to resist pleas for their own phone.

So how can you increase your children's brainpower by improving their diet?

LECITHIN

Research in the 1970s concluded that certain nutrients play a major role in stimulating brain function. The key player was found to be lecithin.

This contains phosphatidyl choline, a substance that conveys nerve impulses from one nerve cell to another. Lecithin granules are available from health food stores and can be sprinkled on cereal, but do check with a nutritionist before giving any supplement to your child. Good natural sources are egg yolks, liver, nuts, whole wheat, soya beans, unrefined vegetable oils and corn.

ZINC

It has long been known that zinc is an essential trace element needed for normal growth and development. Many animal studies have demonstrated that zinc deficiency causes impairments in learning, and research has also shown that zinc can enhance mental capabilities in undernourished children. The nature of zinc's involvement in brain function, however, had been unclear until recent work revealed that zinc is embedded within structures that are absolutely critical for nerve cell activity.

Although zinc is available in a wide variety of foods, marginal deficiencies are common. One reason for this may be poor soil condition, which affects plants' ability to take up zinc. This is passed along the food chain to animals and humans.

The best sources of dietary zinc are oysters (ten times more than other foods), poultry, liver and other

Pineapple, Soya Milk & Wheatgerm *Smoothie*

This recipe contains the perfect threesome to give your child's brain a boost. Pineapple contains manganese, soya milk is rich in lecithin and the wheatgerm is a good source of vitamin E. *Serves 2*

● 180 kcals ● 21 g carbohydrate
● 14 g protein ● 7 g fat ● 7 g fibre

125 g (4 oz) pineapple, chopped
500 ml (17 fl oz) soya milk
2 tablespoons raw wheatgerm
a few ice cubes
ground cinnamon, to decorate (optional)

1 *Put all the ingredients into a food processor or blender and whiz until smooth.*

2 *Pour the smoothie into tall glasses and sprinkle with cinnamon, if you like.*

For more brain power recipes see page 106 ▶▶

meat sources, wheatgerm, lima beans, yogurt, maple syrup and molasses. White bread has much of the zinc content removed; once again, breads made with wholewheat flours are a much better choice for you and your children.

OTHER KEY BRAIN NUTRIENTS

Other nutrients involved with brain function are:
Manganese: This helps the body produce the neurotransmitter choline.
Vitamin E: This is necessary for oxygenation of the brain. Do not forget that cooking and food processing cause a loss of vitamin E in foods. Processed grains lose up to 80 per cent of their vitamin E content, and even freezing destroys much of the vitamin.

Vitamin E is made up of substances called tocopherols, and these are manufactured by plants and are most common in vegetable oils. Wheatgerm oil is the richest, healthiest food source. Animal sources come indirectly from their consumption of plants and the storage of vitamin E in fat tissue.
Phosphorus and sulphur: These work together in the body to produce lecithin.
Omega-3 fatty acids: Contain vital brain nutrients.

The foods to increase if you want more of these brain-empowering nutrients are oily fish, such as tuna, salmon, herrings and mackerel, nuts and seeds, cold-pressed oils such as olive oil, egg yolks, soya beans, whole grains, raw wheatgerm, legumes, brewer's yeast, organ meats, milk and milk products.

And one more thing: the other vital factor in brain function is something else that stimulates the supply of oxygen to the brain – exercise.

67

Foods for
GROWTH

One of the most worrying facts to come to light from recent nutritional studies was the impact of malnourishment on children's growth. If a child is not eating a balanced diet with all the key nutrients, their growth can actually be stunted. A healthy diet is important to all of us, but never is it more important than in your children's early years when their bodies are growing and developing.

The key elements in growth are consumption of sufficient protein and calcium.

PROTEIN

Proteins are the building blocks of the body; muscles, skin tissue, hormones, enzymes, antibodies and blood all need protein for their construction. The first signs of a protein deficiency are falling hair, brittle nails, rough skin, poor muscle tone and anaemia. If the diet is deficient for too long, stunted growth and swelling of the joints will occur.

The main sources of protein are meat, poultry, fish, soya bean products, eggs, milk and milk products and whole grains. Ideally, 15–25 per cent of a child's diet should be a combination of these.

If there is a dietary deficiency of protein, it will affect the other major nutrient involved in growth – calcium. The reason for this is that too little protein results in too little bile being produced in the gut and this will lead to poor absorption of fats. This in turn leads to poorly dissolved fats combining with calcium and iron, which means that the gut cannot absorb those minerals. This will cause constipation and, more importantly, can lead to porous bones and decaying teeth.

CALCIUM

Calcium is the major constituent of our bones and teeth. These absorb calcium into their structure and, like any other tissue in the human body, their cells are continually being broken down and re-formed. Calcium is found in milk and milk products, leafy green vegetables, tofu, soya beans, almonds, sesame seeds, fish and molasses.

In order to be used by the body, calcium needs the presence of the minerals phosphorus and magnesium, and also vitamin D, which is found in oily fish, milk and eggs.

The key substances to avoid so that calcium can do its job are oxalates, which are found in rhubarb, sorrel and spinach. These inhibit the absorption of calcium and can create kidney stones. If eaten in excess, the body utilizes calcium to bind with the oxalates and prevent them entering the bloodstream, diverting it away from its primary role of strengthening the bones and teeth.

Children require between 800 mg and 1,500 mg of calcium per day. To give you an idea of how much calcium certain foods contain, here are the values for its key sources:

250 ml (8 fl oz) glass of milk	300 mg
50 g (2 oz) Swiss cheese	530 mg
175 g (6 oz) yogurt	300 mg
50 g (2 oz) sardines with bones	240 mg
175 g (6 oz) cooked turnip greens	220 mg
75 g (3 oz) almonds	210 mg
175 g (6 oz) tofu	175 mg

Soya products and green vegetables are vital for vegetarians and vegans, who can often be deficient in protein and calcium. Also remember to have a high intake of whole grains and legumes to provide complete proteins.

Banana & Chocolate
Fool

If you want to make this recipe even healthier, you can replace the chocolate with carob. The tofu is a very good growth food, as it is rich in both protein and calcium. The bananas contain vitamin B6, which helps in the metabolism of protein and even helps to conserve it in the body. **Serves 4**

- **280 kcals** ● **32 g carbohydrate**
- **12 g protein** ● **12 g fat** ● **2 g fibre**

500 g (1 lb) silken tofu, roughly chopped
2 ripe bananas, roughly chopped
100 g (3½ oz) chocolate chips or plain chocolate, broken into squares
2 tablespoons orange juice

1 *Put the tofu and bananas into a food processor or blender and blend until smooth.*

2 *Put the chocolate into a small heatproof bowl and melt it over a saucepan of hot water.*

3 *Add the chocolate to the banana and tofu mixture and blend well. Add the orange juice and blend again until all the ingredients are combined.*

4 *Pour the mixture into individual glasses, cover and chill in the refrigerator for 3 hours.*

A neat idea

The fool can be frozen. Place in a suitable container and keep for up to two months. Defrost in the fridge until it is the right consistency or serve semi-frozen as an ice cream substitute.

For more growth recipes see page 110 ▶▶

Foods to boost the immune SYSTEM

The healthier your child, the less chance there is that they will fall prey to every bug being passed around the classroom, and a strong immune system will help them be more resistant to disease and chronic illness in later life. Your children are surrounded by germs every day of their lives, and in order to deal with these, the human body needs to be very resourceful. Luckily, it has a great trick up its sleeve that will fight off viruses, bacteria and other unwanted visitors. This is known as the immune system. If your child is not eating a balanced diet containing the correct proportions of certain vitamins and minerals, then the immune system will take a tumble, and all those germs will be able to get a hold on the body.

THE IMMUNE SYSTEM

In its most simple form, the immune system works on two levels. The skin, stomach acid, friendly bacteria in the gut, urine and tears act as a first line of defence against unwanted germs. Then, on a cellular level, white blood cells called lymphocytes travel around the body on the lookout for any bacteria, viruses or other infecting agents that have managed to get in. Once they have found a foreign body, lymphocytes produce antibodies and toxins that will destroy it. Then they surround the germ and digest it. (You will know this is happening when inflammation occurs.)

Above: Children are surrounded by the germs that cause colds all the time. How well they ward them off depends on the strength of their immune systems.

70

If your child is not eating a balanced diet containing the correct proportions of certain vitamins and minerals, then the immune system will take a tumble …

Lymphocytes travel around the body in the lymphatic system, which is an internal network of vessels that contain lymphatic fluid, or lymph. In order to circulate effectively the lymph relies on activity and exercise to move around the body. At certain points on the lymphatic system there are cell storage houses called lymph nodes. These often become swollen when there is an infection present in the body. The tonsils, adenoids and appendix are all part of the body's lymphatic system.

The thymus gland, bone marrow and spleen are a bit like colleges for immune cells. It is here that lymphocytes mature and are taught which are the good cells and the bad cells, preventing them from attacking their own cells. Sometimes this does go wrong and can result in autoimmune diseases such as diabetes and rheumatoid arthritis.

A DIET TO SUPPORT THE IMMUNE SYSTEM

It is vital that your child takes in sufficient nutrients to support the immune system, and there are certain nutrients that are fundamental to this process:

Vitamin A: This is found in fish oils and liver.

Beta-carotene: This is abundant in root vegetables such as carrots and sweet potatoes, also leafy green vegetables and yellow fruits, such as apricots.

B complex vitamins: Good sources are brewer's yeast, whole grains and raw wheatgerm.

Vitamin C: The best sources are citrus fruits and juices, broccoli and other leafy green vegetables.

Vitamin E: This is found in nuts, seeds, unrefined oils and wheatgerm.

Iron: Red meat, egg yolks, whole grains and leafy green vegetables are all rich in iron.

Zinc: This is found in poultry, oysters, brewer's yeast, raw wheatgerm, egg yolks and seeds.

Below: Beta-carotene, found in orange-coloured fruit and vegetables, is one of the nutrients fundamental to the support of the immune system.

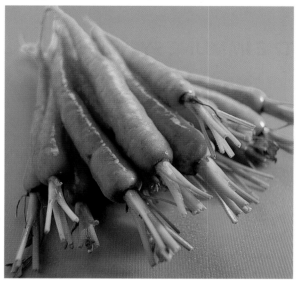

SIGNS OF A WEAKENED IMMUNE SYSTEM

★ **Regular colds, sniffles or flu**
★ **Inability to shake off a cold or other infection**
★ **Easily stressed**
★ **Anxiety or depression**
★ **Food allergies and intolerances**
★ **Hay fever**
★ **Regular use of antibiotics**
★ **Sore throats**
★ **Headaches**

If your child has three of the above symptoms, then the immune system needs some support. If they have five or more of the above, then their immune system is severely over taxed and in need of immediate attention.

Selenium: Nuts, especially brazil nuts, seeds and whole grains are rich sources of selenium.
Calcium: The best sources are milk and dairy products, soya products, leafy green vegetables and sunflower seeds.
Magnesium: This mineral is found in nuts, seeds, figs, apples and leafy green vegetables.

Many of these vitamins and minerals support the immune system by acting as powerful antioxidants, antiviral and antibacterial agents, and antihistamines. They are also essential in the maintenance of the lymphatic glands and nodes and in assisting in the production of white blood cells and antibodies. Some support the metabolism and in the conversion of essential fatty acids into anti-inflammatory prostaglandins, and others guard against the damage caused by pollution.

All of these actions are vital for good health. Antioxidants, for example, protect the body against damage by free radicals. These are substances that are produced all the time by the body's metabolism and as a result of pollution, radiation and sunlight, and if they are allowed to build up in the body they can cause degenerative disease. Key antioxidants are vitamins A, C and E, beta-carotene and the minerals zinc and selenium. All orange, red, purple, yellow and green fruits and vegetables, as well as potatoes, nuts, seeds, wheatgerm, garlic and onions, shellfish, poultry, whole grains, liver, eggs, lean meat and full-fat dairy produce are rich in these antioxidants.

Another area in which our immune systems rely on the nutrients in our food is in the metabolism of fats. Essential fatty acids from the diet – omega-3 and omega-6 fats – are converted in the presence of certain vitamins and minerals into hormone-like substances called prostaglandins. These act to regulate the activity of the white blood cells, which, as we have seen, are vital in the body's defence

Below: Berries contain high levels of antioxidants, which protect against infection and disease.

Orange, Strawberry & Kiwifruit
Juice

This juice packs a mighty antiviral punch, as it is bursting with vitamin C.
Serves 1

- 201 kcals ● 39.5 g carbohydrate
- 6.1 g protein ● 0.6 g fat ● trace fibre

2 oranges, divided into segments
1 kiwifruit, roughly chopped, one piece reserved for decoration
200 g (7 oz) strawberries

1 *Juice the orange segments, kiwifruit and strawberries. Serve immediately in a tall glass decorated with a chunk of kiwifruit.*

A neat idea

Pour the juice into ice lolly containers or ice cube containers, then, once frozen, transfer to freezer bags. Either eat frozen, as lollies, or whiz the cubes in a blender with other fruit to give an added boost to fruit smoothies. Will freeze for 2 months.

system against colds, infections and allergies. Because the body is unable to produce essential fatty acids itself, it is important to include them in the diet. Key sources of essential fatty acids are cold-pressed oils, nuts, seeds and oily fish, such as salmon, tuna, mackerel, sardines and herrings.

A useful sugar substitute with excellent immune-boosting properties is Manuka or tea tree honey. It has powerful antibacterial and antiviral properties and is good for protection against sore throats and colds. You should note, though, that honey should never be given to babies under one year old as there is a risk of botulism.

The message, it would seem, is very clear. In order to give children the best possible chance to stay well and avoid disease, you have to make sure that plenty of the foods listed above are included in their diet. Once you start incorporating more healthy food into their lives, you will be surprised how little room there is left for the junk foods.

For more immune-boosting recipes see page 114 ▶▶

Winter
WARMERS

Your children need all the immune-boosting help they can get at the onset of winter, particularly if they are at school, where there are more 'bugs' flying around than in the insect house at your local zoo. If you do not want your children to be 'under the weather', then you will have to remain vigilant about ensuring they are properly topped up with the right nutrients.

Even though most doctors will tell you that there is no causal link between cold weather and colds, there are many factors to take into account that may lessen your child's resistance to bacterial and viral infections in winter. For example, cold weather tends to keep us indoors more, which restricts the amount of exercise your child may be taking. Also, you will find that crowded public places are often overheated and poorly ventilated, which means that germs can breed and be spread more easily. While outside, the air humidity is usually low in the winter, which may lead to drying out of mucous membranes in the upper respiratory tract, leaving a child more vulnerable to infection. The wind chill factor adds greatly to the loss of body heat, which is the main cause of feeling cold.

Above: Exercise is just as important for your children in winter as it is in summer. Wrap them up warmly so that body heat is maintained.

EFFECTS ON THE BODY

There is no doubt that cold weather has an impact on the body: it affects the respiratory rate and the body's overall metabolic rate – the speed of the vital bodily processes. Body heat is dissipated relatively fast, thus using more energy, so the body will need a bit of extra fuel to cope with this. Hot weather has the opposite effect. When the temperature drops suddenly, conditions such as asthma can worsen. Bronchitis can take a hold if there is a lot of fog and air pollution. Changes in the weather also affect the body's heat-regulating mechanism, the condition of the mucous membranes and the strength of the cold virus. These can all increase infections, particularly if there is a sudden shift from very cold to slightly warmer weather. In the UK the susceptibility to colds and flu increases from September onwards and reaches a peak in February and March.

Another condition, which affects around 2 per cent of people in Northern Europe every year, is seasonal affective disorder, more commonly known as SAD or winter blues. From as early as September, and right through to April, the sufferer will complain of various symptoms including depression, sleep problems and lethargy, and many young people who experience this syndrome will have accompanying behavioural problems.

The problem stems from the lack of bright light in the winter, which alters brain chemistry. Sufferers lose the natural rhythm that signals the body to fall asleep and wake up at the proper times. In the winter we produce more melatonin, a hormone secreted by the light-sensitive pineal gland. This makes us more sleepy and slows us down in the absence of bright daylight, which signals the pineal gland to shut off melatonin production and allows the body to come awake. Obviously, escaping to sunnier climes during the winter months would be the perfect answer to this condition, although it is not a very practical one for most people.

Many people benefit from using a specialist light box, which produces full-spectrum light, and from upping their levels of the neurotransmitter serotonin,

Below: Air humidity is often low in winter, making children more open to upper respiratory tract infections.

which is produced in the body by the amino acid tryptophan and helps to keep us feeling positive. Good dietary sources of tryptophan are pumpkin and sunflower seeds, milk, fish, turnip greens, bananas, potatoes, seaweed, avocados, wheatgerm and chicken.

Another important factor during the winter months is to get out and take some exercise early in the morning in order to literally 'tell' the body to stop producing melatonin.

PROTECTING YOUR CHILD FROM WINTER MISERY

Keeping your child well wrapped up against the winter winds is obviously vital to prevent loss of body heat, and it is equally important to keep them stocked up with lots of warming food and drinks. Do not forget sufficient raw foods such as juices and even salad vegetables as accompaniments to their meals. Vegetables can be included in sandwiches to ensure adequate vitamins and minerals, and maybe you should consider giving your child a comprehensive children's multivitamin.

BREAKFAST

A good hearty breakfast will set children off on the right track, and even though you may be pushed for time, just putting some hot milk on your children's cereal or making them some porridge will give them the start they need. Make sure they drink some vitamin-rich juice and encourage them to have a herbal tea such as blackcurrant with a spoonful of honey, or maybe a cup of hot carob (see the recipe opposite). They will be walking out of a warm house into the cold morning air, and there is nothing more miserable than feeling cold before you have even started your day. Good hot breakfasts could include:

Above: A hearty breakfast such as these power pancakes (see page 118) is even more vital in winter.

★ Scrambled, poached or boiled eggs with wholemeal toast.
★ Porridge.
★ Cheese omelette served with grilled tomatoes.
★ Sweet or savoury pancakes.
★ Hot carob or chocolate drink with croissants and fresh fruit.

LUNCH

If your child is not going to have a hot school meal at lunchtime, then it is time to invest in a good unbreakable vacuum flask. Fill it with steaming hot homemade soup to go with a nutritionally balanced wholemeal roll with cheese and salad and a piece of fresh fruit. This will stand your children in good stead for the rest of the afternoon, and they will need it, especially if they have to brave a freezing cold hockey, football or rugby pitch.

Hot Carob
with Soya Milk & Honey

You could almost kid yourself this is the real thing; it's just as comforting as hot chocolate but without the sugar and caffeine hit.
Serves 1

- 178 kcals ● 34.6 g carbohydrate
- 6.4 g protein ● 2.9 g fat ● .6 g fibre

200 ml (7 fl oz) soya milk
2 teaspoons carob powder
1–2 teaspoons honey

1 *Heat the soya milk in a saucepan until it is nearly boiling. Add the carob powder and honey and stir or whisk until frothy then pour into a mug and serve.*

For more winter-warming recipes see page 118 ▶▶

DINNER

Now is the time to indulge your child with good old hearty fare full of immune-boosting ingredients. The food can still be simple – lots of warming casseroles and stews, roasted winter vegetables and naturally sweetened hot puddings.

At the weekends, wrap children up in warm clothing and get them outside for a brisk walk or a bicycle ride. Exercise is still important to get their circulation going and build their resistance to the dreaded germs.

SNACKS

If your kids like to snack, then remember – the warmer the better. We have already mentioned soup, which is a fantastic way to provide nutritious warming sustenance, but there are plenty of other things you can prepare for them with relatively little effort and that are just as good.

★ Baked potato wedges or other roasted root vegetables such as carrot and sweet potato with dips – you could make a hot tomato salsa or cheese fondue.

★ Toasted sandwiches – try wholemeal bread stuffed with homemade hummus and roasted vegetables, or warm pitta bread filled with hot chicken and fresh coleslaw.

★ Sweet pancakes filled with hot fruit sauce.

★ More hot drinks, such as hot carob (see recipe above), honey and lemon tea with a twist of ginger, yeast extract with hot water, herbal teas or miso soup.

Food allergies &
INTOLERANCE

Nearly everyone has had an adverse reaction to certain foods at some time in their lives, and many people use the term 'allergy' to describe the various symptoms they suffer. But true food allergies are very rare: only 3 per cent of children have clinically proven allergic reactions to foods. Most reactions are, in fact, caused by food intolerances, which are extremely common.

ALLERGIES

An allergic reaction is an immune system response, which can result in the following symptoms:
Mouth: The lips or tongue can swell, and itching can occur to the roof of the mouth and lips.
Digestive tract: An allergic reaction can lead to stomach cramps, vomiting and diarrhoea.
Skin: This can suffer from hives, rashes or eczema.
Airways: Wheezing or breathing problems can occur.

All of this will occur within a few minutes to an hour. It is essential to identify true food allergies and prevent them, because these reactions can cause devastating illness and in some cases can be fatal.

Almost all food allergies are caused by seven foods: milk, eggs, fish and shellfish, wheat, soya and other beans, nuts and peanuts (which are legumes). In children, the most common food allergens are

Above: Allergies to certain foods, or that take the form of asthma, hay fever or hives, are more common in children whose parents suffer from allergies.

eggs, milk and peanuts, and many children will eventually outgrow these allergies, especially to milk and soya.

It is more likely that a child will develop food allergies if both parents suffer from allergies. These do not necessarily have to be food-related, and may perhaps appear as hay fever, asthma or hives.

If you suspect that your child has a food allergy, then the best course of action is to consult a doctor or allergist. They will then determine whether the

In the highly polluted, pesticide- and additive-ridden world we live in, food intolerance is on the increase.

symptoms are consistent with an adverse reaction to specific foods.

If your child is diagnosed as having a serious allergy then one or more of the following actions will be advised:

Elimination diet: This will involve rigorous checking of all foodstuffs to ensure they do not contain the offending ingredients.

Medical alert bracelet: An alert bracelet or necklace can be worn stating your child has a food allergy.

Carrying a syringe of adrenaline: Obtained by prescription from the doctor, a shot of adrenaline (epinephrine) should be administered at the first signs of allergic symptoms to avoid the possibility of an anaphylactic reaction (an extreme allergic reaction that can be fatal).

Immediate medical assistance: Emergency medical attention should be sought in the event of a full-blown allergic reaction.

FOOD INTOLERANCE

As mentioned above, true allergic reactions are very rare, but food intolerance – well, that is another matter. In the highly polluted, pesticide- and additive-ridden world we live in, food intolerance is on the increase. Over 20 million Americans are being treated every year for diet-related problems.

Above: Milk is one of the most common food allergens in children. Children often grow out of this sort of allergy.

In most cases, the trouble is caused by an intolerance to one or more types of foods, which indicates a problem with metabolism. The body cannot digest a certain food because of a chemical imbalance. This can result in bloating, abdominal pain or diarrhoea.

The most common intolerance is lactose intolerance. This affects one in ten people and is caused by a deficiency of lactase, which is an enzyme in the gut that degrades lactose, found in cows' milk and milk products. The body cannot digest the lactose, which is then used by bacteria to produce gas, bloating, pain and sometimes diarrhoea. This is very common in young children, and has been on the increase since more and more women have given up on breast-feeding.

A safe and delicious alternative to dairy milk is a milk made from nuts. Nut milks are incredibly easy to make. As a general rule, you need one part nuts to three parts water: 100 g (3½ oz) nuts to 500 ml (17 fl oz) filtered water provides more than enough for a couple of children at breakfast time. The best nuts to use are almonds and cashews. Simply combine the nuts and water in a food processor or blender and process until smooth. Then strain through a fine sieve or piece of muslin and add a little honey, vanilla or nutmeg. Use in place of milk. You can also use the nut pulp: mix it with a mashed

Below: Children with gluten allergies can consume small amounts of oats. Opt for whole oats to reduce the risk of wheat contamination at the milling stage.

banana, add two or three finely chopped dates, and spread on wholemeal toast, rice cakes or pitta bread.

As discussed earlier, many children have an adverse reaction to additives. Compounds that are most frequently linked to intolerance are yellow dye number 5, monosodium glutamate and sulphites. These can cause asthma-type symptoms such as wheezing and shortness of breath.

Another relatively common intolerance is to gluten, a component of wheat and other grains such as barley and rye. Gluten intolerance is associated with a disease called gluten-sensitive enteropathy or coeliac disease and is caused by an abnormal immune response to gluten. Symptoms include frequent indigestion, abdominal pain, loss of weight, depression and foul-smelling stools.

It has only become known recently that children do not develop the necessary starch-splitting enzymes to deal with cereals until they are between two and three years old. By feeding children on a diet high in wheat and other gluten-rich grains before they have had the chance to develop a tolerance to these foods, a parent could, without realizing it, be increasing the possibility of their child developing coeliac disease.

If you suspect your child has a gluten intolerance, then avoid the following: bread, wheat pasta, flour-based products, malt-based products, processed foods that contain hydrolysed vegetable/plant proteins or textured vegetable proteins, soy sauce, flavourings and the binders and fillers found in some vitamins and medications. There are many gluten-free alternatives to these available in health food shops and some supermarkets.

Recent research has shown that a moderate intake of oats is acceptable for children with a gluten allergy. Buy whole oats and ensure they come from as pure a source as possible, as cross-contamination with wheat may occur at the milling stage.

The following flours are healthy alternatives for those with a gluten intolerance. You can buy all of them separately, or you can buy commercial blends for making bread or cakes.

★ Millet.
★ Rice.
★ Corn.
★ Gram (chick pea).

Some children suffer from exercise-induced food allergies, if they eat a specific type of food before exercising. As their body temperature rises they start to itch, feel lightheaded and soon have allergic reactions such as hives and breathing difficulties. If this is the case, your child should not eat for a couple of hours before exercising.

In general, in order to minimize the possibility of food allergies and intolerance avoid processed, convenience foods, stick to natural alternatives, and buy organic produce if possible. If your child does regularly exhibit any of the symptoms mentioned above, keep a record of the contents of each meal. This will give your doctor more detail and increase the chance of a successful diagnosis.

Honey & Lemon
Roasted Peaches

This is a really delicious pudding that even the most sensitive of little stomachs should be able to handle. Why not serve it with dairy-free ice cream for a special treat? Peaches contain antioxidants, lemon is rich in vitamin C, and honey is reputedly good for hay fever.
Serves 4–6

● 85 kcals ● 21.3 g carbohydrate
● 1.5 g protein ● 0.1 g fat ● 0.4 g fibre

6 peaches, halved and stoned
3 tablespoons honey
juice of 1 lemon
dairy-free ice cream or yogurt, to serve (optional)
chopped mint, to garnish

1 *Put the peaches, cut side up, into a lightly buttered ovenproof dish and drizzle a little honey and lemon juice into each cavity. Bake in a pre-heated oven, 200°C (400°F), Gas Mark 6, for about 20 minutes.*

2 *Serve with dairy-free ice cream or yogurt, if liked, and sprinkle with a little chopped mint.*

A neat idea

Bananas and figs can also be cooked in this way.

For more intolerance and allergy recipes see page 122 ▶▶

Foods for the
SICK CHILD

Even if you are a paragon of virtue on the nutrition front, from time to time your children will succumb to the odd germ. And so they should – if their immune systems do not get in a bit of practice on the odd minor ailment, they will never develop sufficiently enough to take on the big stuff.

Usually when a child is ill it is as a result of a common viral infection such as cold or flu, a bacterial bout, such as ear and chest infection, or those familiar childhood ailments, chickenpox and measles.

Having said that, you should be vigilant about spotting the difference between a common cold and

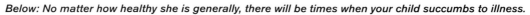

Below: No matter how healthy she is generally, there will be times when your child succumbs to illness.

something more serious. If your child ever exhibits a combination of the following symptoms, you must act very quickly as these are all signs of meningitis:

★ Fever.
★ Bad headache.
★ Purple rash that does not disappear when gently pressed with a glass.
★ An aversion to bright lights.
★ Vomiting.
★ Stiff back and neck.

In a baby the symptoms of meningitis are slightly different:

★ Fever.
★ Crying.
★ A bulging fontanelle.
★ Intolerance of bright lights.
★ Fits or loss of consciousness.
★ Purple rash.

FEVERS

When a child is ill, the infection is often accompanied by a fever. This is quite normal and quite necessary. The temperature rises as the body goes into healing overdrive and tries to rid itself of the offending germs.

Above: When your child has a fever, give her plenty of natural fluids and extra vitamin C. Oranges fit the bill on both counts.

At this stage, the sick child should go to bed with plenty of natural fluids, such as water and fruit juice, as it is vital they do not get dehydrated. It is usually beneficial at this stage to give them some extra vitamin C.

If the symptoms do not abate, get worse or are accompanied by severe drowsiness, rashes and violent vomiting, call the doctor. Whatever the immune system is trying to do, it is not working.

ANTIBIOTICS

The general trend in the modern world is to rely on medication and not concentrate on prevention. People are being prescribed antibiotics whether they need them or not, and this overuse is creating new breeds of super-bugs that are resistant to any antibiotics that are thrown at them. In the long term, we are suppressing our immune systems. Antibiotics

Above: Antibiotics destroy all bacteria in the gut. Live natural yogurt is a good way to replenish some of the friendly bacteria your child needs.

BRONCHITIS AND TONSILLITIS

When you hear an 'itis' word, it means something is inflamed. The two most common complaints seen in children are bronchitis and tonsillitis. If your child's temperature starts to climb and they begin to have coughing fits and to spit up mucus, this means that there is inflammation of the bronchial tubes, the two large tubes that branch off the windpipe. Bronchitis can be caused by wayward bacteria from the throat or by the same virus that caused the initial cold or flu. As the lining of those tubes swells, mucus builds up. The coughing is a sign that your children are trying to clear that mucus from their bronchial passages.

If the bronchitis is caused by bacteria, your doctor may prescribe an antibiotic. If it is a viral infection, this will not help, but you can do a lot to make your child more comfortable and maybe even better faster.

Tonsillitis is a highly infectious inflammation of the tonsils, two tissue masses at the back of the throat. It is usually caused by a virus, but can be the result of bacteria called streptococci, in which case antibiotics may be effective. It usually lasts a couple of days, but if the child starts to cough up green or yellow phlegm, then the infection has probably spread to the chest.

With either bronchitis or tonsillitis, don't make your child eat if they don't want to. They need all their body's resources to fight the infection, and when they are hungry, they will be the first to tell you. Make sure they drink plenty of fluids – water or light fruit juices – and when they are ready to eat, keep it simple and easy to digest. Fruit and fresh fruit and vegetable juices are fantastic, as the vitamins and enzymes act as a natural booster. Then try rice and whole grains, soups and salads, which are all light on the system.

If your child has a cold, flu, bronchitis, or any other infection that produces mucus avoid all dairy products, eggs, sugary and savoury snacks, fried foods and red meat, as they are all mucus-forming.

kill off bacteria, but do not discriminate between the good guys and the bad guys – a course of antibiotics will wipe out a large percentage of the healthy bacteria in the gut, allowing the development of fungal infections such as candida or thrush. One course of antibiotics can destroy the friendly bacteria in your child's gut for anything up to six months.

Think very carefully before allowing your children to take antibiotics and remember, they are not effective against colds and flu, as these are viral infections. Seek natural ways to treat your child and help to build their immune systems. This will be far better for them in the long run, as it will give them greater resistance against infection.

If your child has taken antibiotics, then replenish the probiotics (friendly bacteria) with supplements or live yogurt, containing either acidophilus or bifidus.

Fruit
Kebabs

This is a very easy dish, which is not only good when the apple of your eye is under the weather, but an excellent way to serve fruit all year round. The pineapple contains bromelain, which increases the effectiveness of antibiotics and is a good digestive.

Makes about 16–20 skewers

- 40 kcals ● 9.8 g carbohydrate
- 0.5 g protein ● 0.1 g fat ● 1.3 g fibre

1 mango, peeled and stoned
250 g (8 oz) fresh pineapple
2 large bananas
125 g (4 oz) each black and green seedless grapes
250 g (8 oz) strawberries, hulled
lime juice and honey, to serve (optional)

1 *Chop the mango, pineapple and bananas into chunks about 2.5 cm (1 inch) thick. Thread a piece of each fruit on to each bamboo skewer and arrange on a serving platter. To serve, squeeze a little lime juice over the skewers and drizzle with honey, if wished.*

A neat idea

Serve the fruit kebabs with live yogurt to replenish the healthy bacteria in the bowel destroyed by antibiotics, but don't give yogurt to a child who is producing a lot of mucus, as it will aggravate the condition.

Variation

- 943 kcals ● 17.5 g carbohydrate
- 27 g protein ● 85 g fat ● 6.8 g fibre

As a variation, I really like the combination of fruit and crunchy peanut sauce. To make the sauce, mix 100 g (3½ oz) crunchy peanut butter with 2 tablespoons lemon juice then add 150 ml (¼ pint) coconut milk and stir well. Serve the sauce in a bowl and spoon it over the fruit kebabs.

For more recipes for a sick child see page 126 ▶▶

Diarrhoea & stomach
UPSETS

When your child has diarrhoea, in other words the frequent passage of unformed or watery stools, it is more than just messy, it is also potentially dangerous. This is primarily because diarrhoea depletes the body of fluid, and if that fluid is not replaced, the body will draw from its stores. When that happens, the child runs the risk of dehydration.

Diarrhoea can be the result of dietary factors, such as too much fruit juice or fibre. With babies, the introduction of a new food may be enough to cause an upset. But in many cases the cause is a virus.

Acute diarrhoea is the most common form seen by parents. Although it does not last long, it is more dangerous than the chronic form because it is often accompanied by fever, which increases the likelihood of dehydration. Some children develop chronic non-specific diarrhoea that has no known cause and is usually harmless. At the onset of any diarrhoea, however, it really takes a doctor to tell the difference.

TREATING DIARRHOEA

The most important thing is not to allow dehydration, which will happen if the child is losing more fluid than is being taken in. The main treatment for diarrhoea, therefore, is to provide plenty for the child to drink. This is the most important piece of advice that health professionals have to offer.

Babies up to 10 kg (20 lb) who have diarrhoea and are feverish or vomiting should be drinking about 150 ml of liquid per kg of body weight (3 fl oz per lb) per day to avoid dehydration; children over 10 kg (20 lb) should drink 50–80 ml per kg (1–1½ fl oz per lb) daily. It is best to stick to simple fluids such as water, possibly mixed with a small amount of apple juice.

One remedy that is apparently excellent for diarrhoea or infant colic is to give the child rice milk, which is available from health food stores, or rice water. You can make this by boiling rice for 15 minutes, straining it and reserving the liquid.

Do not offer milk or milk products, as a lot of children have trouble digesting milk when they are sick. That is because illness frequently causes superficial damage to the intestines and disrupts

Below: The most important treatment for diarrhoea is to drink plenty of water to prevent dehydration.

Yogurt with
Honey &
Carob

normal production of lactase, the enzyme that helps digest the lactose in milk. If your baby is on a cows' milk formula, switch to a soya or hypoallergenic one that does not contain lactose. If your baby is breast-feeding, though, you need to continue breast-feeding as much as you can to keep up his or her strength.

Once the diarrhoea has abated, give your child a probiotic supplement, such as acidophilus or bifidus, or live yogurt if they have no problem with dairy products, as this will normalize the intestinal flora.

CONSTIPATION

If a child has been eating a diet high in refined carbohydrates, and leading a sedentary lifestyle with not enough exercise, then constipation can easily result. This can lead to a lot of discomfort and even a reluctance to go to the toilet in case it is painful.

Avoid constipation by cutting out junk foods and replacing with whole grains and plenty of raw fruit and vegetables, and ensuring that your child is drinking enough water.

If your child has got constipation then try making porridge and including a teaspoon of flaxseeds or psyllium seeds. These contain a fibre called mucilage, which absorbs a great deal of fluid in the gut making the seeds swell. They add bulk to stools, which makes them press on the colon wall, triggering the

This easy-to-eat snack is great for children who have had a bad tummy. The yogurt restores the natural intestinal balance to the digestive system, while the honey has antibacterial properties and works with the carob, which contains tannins that bind to (and thereby inactivate) toxins and inhibit growth of bacteria.
Serves 1

- **249 kcals** ● **41 g carbohydrate**
- **12.8 g protein** ● **6 g fat** ● **0.4 g fibre**

150 g (5 oz) natural live yogurt
1 tablespoon honey
1 tablespoon wheatgerm
1 tablespoon carob powder

1 *Put the yogurt, honey, wheatgerm and carob powder into a food processor or blender and whiz until smooth.*

For more recipes for a child with diarrhoea and stomach upsets see page 130 ▶▶

muscle contractions called peristalsis. Make sure your child drinks plenty of fluids or the stools may obstruct the digestive tract. If your child has asthma, you must not use psyllium, as it can cause an allergic reaction.

Pears, prunes and figs are good for constipation. Try them either whole or juiced. Never give bran to a child as it is too rough for a young digestive system.

Foods to treat
COLDS & FLU

The common cold, an infection of the upper respiratory tract, is caused by any one of 200 different viruses. As the immune system battles against the viral infection, it produces the all-too-familiar symptoms: nasal congestion, runny nose, watery eyes, coughing and sometimes fever.

Most cold viruses are extremely hardy. They can survive for several hours on hands, clothing and hard surfaces, as well as in the air, giving your child ample opportunity to pick up something infectious.

As long as your child has no fever and is eating and sleeping well despite the cold, you can treat the condition very well at home. However, if the symptoms worsen, if there is a low-grade fever (37.8–38.3°C/100–101°F) for a few days or if the fever suddenly gets higher, it is time for a visit to the doctor as your child may have a bacterial infection rather than a cold.

If your child's runny nose and cough have not improved after ten days, your child may have a sinus infection, which may follow a cold because the sinuses become inflamed and cannot drain properly. In this case a visit to the doctor may be the best course of action.

Luckily, there are some good natural remedies on your side in the fight against colds and flu:

★ Garlic contains several helpful compounds, including allicin, one of the plant kingdom's most potent, broad-spectrum antibiotics, and regular consumption of garlic can help prevent colds and flu. You know the effect that garlic has on your breath? Well, this herb's aromatic compounds are readily released from the lungs and respiratory tract, putting garlic's active ingredients right where they can be most effective against cold viruses. Garlic can be added to soups and sauces and many children love garlic bread.

★ Ginger contains nearly a dozen antiviral compounds. Pouring a cup of boiling water on to

Below: Fresh pineapple juice is great for colds because it has a high level of vitamin C and breaks down mucus.

Honey & Lemon
Tea

This is an old favourite for sore throats and runny noses. Honey and lemon are a perfect mixture of soothing and antibacterial ingredients.
Serves 1

- 100 kcals ● 26 g carbohydrate
- 0.2 g protein

juice of ½ lemon
2 teaspoons honey

1 *Put the lemon juice into a beaker. Add the honey and top up with 150 ml (¼ pint) hot water.*

A neat idea

You could add a few slivers of fresh root ginger, which is excellent for treating a chesty cough.

For more cold and flu recipes see page 134 ▶▶

a couple of tablespoons of fresh, shredded ginger root is a great cold treatment. Scientists have isolated several chemicals (sesquiterpenes) in ginger that have specific effects against the most common family of cold viruses, the rhinoviruses. Some of these chemicals are remarkably potent in their antirhinovirus effects. Ginger also contains gingerols and shogaols, which help to relieve cold symptoms because they reduce pain and fever, suppress coughing and have a mild sedative effect that encourages rest.

★ Onion is a close relative of garlic and contains many similar antiviral chemicals. One old folk remedy for colds recommends steeping raw onion slices overnight in honey, then taking the resulting mixture at intervals like a cough syrup.

★ Fresh pineapple juice is wonderful for colds and flu as it contains high levels of vitamin C. It also breaks down mucus. To treat a cold, drink 125–175 ml (4–6 fl oz) of juice diluted with the same amount of water at least four times a day.

★ Increase your child's intake of vitamin C-rich foods, such as citrus fruits and blackcurrants.

★ A good zinc supplement will zap the cold.

★ For anyone suffering from a cold or flu, make immune-boosting soups with plenty of garlic and onion, fresh vegetables and chicken, which is excellent at breaking down mucus.

Avoid the following foods like the proverbial plague as these will increase mucus production and delay your child getting over the cold or flu:

★ All dairy products and eggs.
★ Fried food.
★ Red meat.
★ Sugary and salty snacks.

Common childhood
AILMENTS

We all remember being at home sick and off school, and just how miserable it is, particularly with things like earache, toothache and, even worse, chickenpox. The worst bit is when you are starting to feel a bit better. I tend to think that either picky or comfort food works best, especially when your child is trying to get his or her appetite back on track. The recipes suggested on page 93 and on pages 138–41 should tempt their taste buds and do them the power of good.

CHICKENPOX

Chickenpox is a fairly harmless malady that can strike people of any age, from babies to adults. For a week or more, the discomfort is almost continuous. First there may be mild fever, then come the blisters, the itching and, finally, the scabbing. In very rare cases, chickenpox can develop into more serious ailments (see page 91).

The best way to reduce the discomfort and itchiness is to dress your child lightly in cotton clothing or pyjamas. The cooler you can keep your child's skin in the first 48–72 hours, the better. Avoid bundling your child up. Cotton is the best choice because it is the least irritating to the skin.

Another way to lower your child's temperature is to bathe the skin with a cool cloth or put the child in a cool bath. It is important to make sure, though, that the water is not so cold that your child shivers.

You could also try an itch-relieving bath: grind a handful of oatmeal and put it into lukewarm water. Or soothe with soda: baking soda is a good substitute for oatmeal. Stir about half a cup of baking soda into a shallow bath or a full cup into a deep bath. Use a flannel to spread the bathwater over all affected areas of skin. If your child has one or two spots that are particularly itchy, soak a flannel in cool water, then wring it out and lay it on the affected area for five minutes and repeat as often as needed.

Keep your child fresh and clean. Children with chickenpox should have a daily shower and shampoo to keep the sores clean and help prevent infection, and you should change their clothes daily to reduce the risk of the sores getting infected.

Try to control the scratching. If your child is old enough to understand, explain that he or she should not scratch, because that can cause infection or scarring. If the itching is so bad that the child simply cannot ignore it, offer a cool wet flannel to gently scratch the skin with.

Another thing to remember is to trim your child's fingernails as soon as the first signs of chickenpox strike. Scratching with sharp nails can lead to a bacterial infection in the sores, which can result in permanent scarring.

I tend to think that either picky or comfort food works best, especially when your child is trying to get his or her appetite back on track.

Above: Chickenpox blisters can be extremely itchy. Try to discourage or control scratching as much as possible.

When to see the doctor

In rare cases, the chickenpox virus can cause encephalitis, and it has also been linked to Reye's syndrome. Both ailments are life-threatening brain inflammations, so give your doctor a call if you have any doubts about your child's symptoms. Always contact your doctor when your child has:

★ Fever after the sores have begun to scab over.
★ High fever accompanied by severe headache, vomiting, disorientation or convulsions.
★ Pain when the neck is stretched.

You should also contact the doctor if your child has more than a few sores that are excessively swollen, red or painful. These may be infected and antibiotics may be necessary.

EARACHE

Earache is usually the result of a cold, when the Eustachian tube (the pencil-sized canal that leads from the back of your nasal passages to your ear) becomes congested. Since there is less air in the middle ear, it creates a negative pressure, sometimes associated with fluid accumulation. Because of this, your child will not feel sharp pain in his or her ear, but will feel discomfort or pressure within it or have muffled hearing.

Pain can also occur in the ear when the Eustachian tube becomes inflamed or congested from an allergy or sore throat.

One way to relieve the pain of earache is to use warmth. Gentle heat promotes blood flow and marshals infection-fighting white blood cells in the area. Prepare a hot-water bottle, a hot towel or a heating pad, warmed to a comfortably hot level and wrapped in a towel. Keep the heat held against your child's ear for 20 minutes or until the pain goes away, whichever comes first.

When to see a doctor

See your doctor as soon as possible if your child's ear pain is:

★ Severe.
★ Accompanied by drainage or discharge from the ear.
★ Accompanied by a fever of 39°C (102°F) or higher.
★ Not accompanied by a cold.
★ Not caused by water in the ear.

TOOTHACHE

A toothache can be caused by any number of problems. While it could be a cavity, there could also be a crack in the enamel, a permanent tooth trying to break through, an irritated gum or just a loose baby tooth causing discomfort.

Because you probably do not know for sure what is causing your child's tooth to hurt, the experts suggest that you try as many of the following remedies as necessary to help ease your child's pain during the hours you must wait before he or she can see the dentist.

★ Look for the obvious. Sometimes a piece of food can become jammed between two teeth and cause soreness. Look carefully in the area where your child has pain to see if anything is stuck there. If you can see something carefully try to

Below: Earache is a symptom of the common cold. Help relieve it by holding a wrapped hot towel against the ear.

Banana
Popsicles

When your child is stuck at home getting over measles or chickenpox and is in need of a little treat for being good, these nutritious snacks are just the ticket.
Makes 6

● **232 kcals** ● **20.7 g carbohydrate**
● **4.9 g protein** ● **14.8 g fat** ● **3.8 g fibre**

3 bananas
100 g (3½ oz) peanut butter, softened
50 g (2 oz) chopped peanuts, walnuts, sunflower
  or sesame seeds

1 *Cut the bananas in half widthways, and push a lolly stick into the cut end of each half. Spread the bananas with peanut butter and roll them in the nuts or seeds.*

2 *Wrap the lollies individually in waxed paper and freeze for 3 hours.*

A neat idea

These popsicles can be frozen for up to 2 months. Eat frozen.

remove the material with dental floss, or let your child try to do it if he or she is old enough. (Children aged seven or eight can usually manage the floss themselves.)

★ Try a saltwater rinse. If you can see that the gum is a bit swollen or irritated, a warm saltwater rinse may be the ticket to relief. Mix a teaspoon of salt in a glass of hot water, then let it cool slightly until it is warm. Your child should swish the warm saltwater around and spit it out. Repeat this every few hours.

★ Apply an ice pack. If the pain is severe, a cold pack may numb the pain and provide relief. Wrap a bag of crushed ice in a towel and hold it against the painful jaw.

★ Choose soft, lukewarm foods or liquids. A painful tooth can feel even worse if your child chomps down on it while eating. Opt for soup, broth or anything soft, but avoid very hot foods. If cold irritates the tooth, avoid cold drinks.

★ Select bland foods. If the problem appears to be an irritated gum, spicy foods could make it more painful. Stay away from vinegar, mustard and salt, for example, because they could irritate the area. You should also skip sugary foods or juice, because if the problem is a cavity, sugar will make the pain even worse.

For more recipes for common childhood ailments see page 138 ▶▶

Foods that
ENERGIZE

Hopping Frog Smoothie
with Spirulina

This bright green cocktail is a positive sea of nutrients. The banana is a good source of potassium and vitamin B6, kiwifruits are rich in vitamin C and spirulina is one of the rare plant foods to supply all the essential amino acids; it also provides a usable form of vitamin B12. This smoothie will definitely leave your child full of bounce.
Serves 2

1 *Put the banana, kiwifruits, spirulina and apple juice into a food processor or blender with a few ice cubes and blend until smooth.*

2 *Divide between two tall glasses and serve immediately.*

- 227 kcals ● 53 g carbohydrate
- 1.5 g protein ● 9 g fat
- 2.8 g fibre

1 banana, chopped
2 kiwifruits, chopped
1 tablespoon spirulina
600 ml (1 pint) apple juice
a few ice cubes

Get Up & Go
Muesli

This breakfast is bursting with energy-boosting goodies, which will give your child a great start to the day and sustain them until lunch. It is full of protein, carbohydrates, fibre, vitamins B6, C and E, calcium, folic acid … I could go on and on extolling its virtues. And, if you pile some fresh fruit on the top, then you will be adding even more goodness. Incidentally, the nuts make up a major part of the calorie count of this recipe, accounting for 580 of the 784 kcals.

Serves 1

1 *Put the soya milk into a bowl and add the cereal flakes and raisins. Cover the bowl and leave the muesli to soak overnight in the refrigerator.*

2 *Next morning, stir in the yogurt, grated apple, orange juice and nuts. Mix in the wheatgerm and drizzle with honey. Top the muesli with fresh fruit such as banana and raspberries, if you like.*

75 ml (3 fl oz) soya milk
50 g (2 oz) oatmeal, wheat or rye flakes
25 g (1 oz) raisins
50 g (2 oz) natural yogurt
1 apple, grated
juice of ½ orange
25 g (1 oz) chopped mixed nuts – almonds, walnuts, brazils, hazelnuts, cashews
25 g (1 oz) wheatgerm
1 teaspoon honey
fresh fruit (optional)

Some neat ideas

If your child prefers a crunchier cereal, omit the soaking and mix all the ingredients just before serving.

Instead of raisins, try dried apricots, dates, figs, prunes, peaches or sour cherries for a bit of variety.

- **784 kcals** ● **112 g carbohydrate**
- **18.3 g protein** ● **55 g fat**
- **6 g fibre**

Wok
Around the Clock
Stir-Fry

This is a good dinner for children who need to keep on the go. It will provide an instant boost as it is full of energy-giving vegetables, but it won't slow them down since the vegetables are all easily digestible.
Serves 2

1 *Chop the mangetout, red pepper, carrot and spring onions into fine strips. Slice the chicken into strips 1 cm (½ inch) wide.*

2 *Heat the oil in a wok or large frying pan. Add the chicken and cook, stirring, over a high heat for about 5 minutes until it is golden brown. Add the mangetout, pepper, carrots, spring onions, baby corn, broccoli and crushed garlic cloves and cook for 1–2 minutes. Turn the heat down to medium, cover with a lid and cook for a further 3–4 minutes.*

3 *Stir in the tamari sauce and sesame oil and serve immediately. For a more substantial and balanced meal, serve the stir-fry on a bed of rice noodles.*

- 362 kcals ● 6.1 g carbohydrate
- 36 g protein ● 21 g fat
- 6.7 g fibre

50 g (2 oz) mangetout
50 g (2 oz) red pepper
50 g (2 oz) carrot
2 spring onions
300 g (10 oz) boneless, skinless chicken breast
2 tablespoons corn or groundnut oil
50 g (2 oz) baby corn or frozen sweetcorn
50 g (2 oz) small broccoli florets
2 garlic cloves, crushed
1 teaspoon tamari sauce
1 teaspoon sesame oil
rice noodles, to serve (optional)

A neat idea

If your little ones aren't meat-eaters – or just to ring the changes – try substituting tofu or salmon fillet for the chicken.

Foods for
SPORTS

Leek & Potato
Soup

This soup is particularly good for those cold winter games days out on the pitch. You can send your child off to school with a flask full of soup, a wholemeal roll and a piece of fruit and know that they will have enough fuel to get them through the toughest of games.
Serves 6

1 *Melt the butter in a large saucepan and sauté the leeks, potato and carrot for about 5 minutes, stirring occasionally.*

2 *Add the stock and bring it to the boil, then reduce the heat, cover the pan and simmer for 20 minutes.*

3 *Leave the soup to cool slightly then purée in a food processor or blender, in batches if necessary.*

4 *Return the soup to the pan, then taste and adjust the seasoning. Stir in the soya milk and heat it through but without letting it boil.*

● 102 kcals ● 7.5 g carbohydrate
● 4 g protein ● 6 g fat
● 2 g fibre

25 g (1 oz) butter
500 g (1 lb) leeks, chopped into
   2 cm (¾ inch) slices
1 potato, cut into cubes
1 carrot, cut into cubes
1.2 litres (2 pints) vegetable stock
150 ml (¼ pint) soya milk
salt and pepper (optional)

A neat idea

This soup can be frozen. After you have blended it, allow it to cool and freeze in a microwavable container. If storage is limited in the freezer, halve the amount of liquid used. Either defrost in a microwave or at room temperature. Add the remaining liquid, if necessary, and reheat in a microwave or over a pan of boiling water, adding the soya milk and seasoning. Will freeze for up to six months.

Go Faster
Pasta
with
Fresh Tomato & Basil Sauce

If you want your child to stay the distance, then this simple but tasty pasta dish will give them all the energy they need. The sauce can be made in advance and frozen to save time. **Serves 4**

1 *First make the tomato sauce. Heat the oil in a large saucepan and slowly sauté the onion and celery until they are well softened.*

2 *Add the garlic, tomatoes, basil and sugar to the pan and cook briskly over a high heat for 10 minutes.*

3 *Leave the sauce to cool, then whiz in a food processor or blender until smooth.*

4 *Return the sauce to the pan and simmer for 10 minutes. Season to taste.*

5 *Meanwhile, cook the pasta according to packet instructions in lots of salted boiling water until al dente. Drain well and toss with the tomato sauce. Serve with grated Parmesan.*

- 694 kcals ● 120 g carbohydrate
- 19 g protein ● 20 g fat
- 18 g fibre

500 g (1 lb) tubular pasta, such as penne or rigatoni
freshly grated Parmesan cheese, to serve

Tomato Sauce
5 tablespoons extra virgin olive oil
1 onion, finely chopped
1 celery stick, finely chopped
2 garlic cloves, crushed
1 kg (2 lb) tomatoes, skinned, deseeded and finely chopped or 2 x 400 g (13 oz) cans Italian plum tomatoes
12 basil leaves
1 teaspoon raw brown sugar
salt and pepper (optional)

A neat idea

Substitute corn, rice, vegetable or millet pasta for wheat pasta if you are allergic to wheat or gluten.

Eggy Bread
with Hot
Bananas, Cinnamon & Honey

- ● 606 kcals ● 75 g carbohydrate
- ● 12 g protein ● 62 g fat
- ● 71 g fibre

4 eggs
3 tablespoons single cream
1 teaspoon ground cinnamon, plus extra
   to serve
4 thick slices wholemeal fruit bread
75 g (3 oz) butter
4 bananas, sliced

To serve
honey or maple syrup
single cream or Greek yogurt (optional)

A neat idea

To make a savoury version of this recipe,
replace the wholemeal fruit bread with
multigrain bread and serve with grilled
tomatoes rather than the bananas and
honey or maple syrup.

This is a great breakfast or teatime treat. It
may seem a little high on the calorie front,
and you may wince at the sight of the cream,
but remember that your little sportsperson
will be burning a lot of energy. This dish
provides all the carbohydrates, vitamin B12
and phosphorus that they will need in order
to put in a good performance.
Serves 4

1 *Put the eggs, cream and cinnamon
into a bowl and beat with a fork, then pour into
a shallow, flat-bottomed dish. Add the bread
and leave to soak for 5 minutes, then turn over
and soak for a further 5 minutes.*

2 *Heat the butter in a non-stick frying
pan. When it is foaming, add the bread to the
pan and cook for 4–5 minutes on each side or
until golden. Put the cooked bread on a heated
serving plate and keep warm in a low oven.*

3 *Add the bananas to the pan and toss
gently for 5 minutes, then spoon them over the
bread. Drizzle the bananas with honey or
maple syrup, dust with cinnamon and serve.
For an extra treat, add a splash of single cream
or Greek yogurt.*

Foods that
CALM

Peking
Duck

I don't know any non-vegetarians who dislike the Peking duck served in Chinese restaurants. I have added shredded lettuce as it is very calming. Duck is a nutritious choice for children as it contains a high level of iron. I have also substituted a sticky date purée for the more traditional hoisin sauce. I call mine No Sin Sauce; it is just as sweet but additive free. You can get rice paper wrappers from oriental supermarkets.
Serves 4

- 564 kcals ● 47 g carbohydrate
- 67 g protein ● 12 g fat ● 6.3 g fibre

1 tablespoon honey
1 tablespoon tamari sauce
4 boneless, skinless duck breasts
4 baby gem lettuces, finely shredded
½ cucumber, sliced into julienne strips
4 spring onions, sliced into julienne strips
16 rice paper wrappers

No Sin Sauce
250 g (8 oz) pitted dates
250 ml (8 fl oz) water
3 teaspoons balsamic vinegar
3 teaspoons sesame oil

1 *Combine the honey and tamari sauce and rub the mixture over the duck breasts. Put them on an oiled baking sheet, cover with foil and bake in a preheated oven, 220°C (425°F), Gas Mark 7, for 20 minutes or until cooked through. Remove the duck from the oven and leave to stand for 5 minutes.*

2 *Meanwhile, make the sauce. Put the dates and water into a small saucepan and simmer for about 10 minutes until the dates are soft. Transfer the mixture into a food processor or blender with the balsamic vinegar and sesame oil and purée until smooth.*

3 *Using a pastry brush, brush both sides of the rice paper wrappers with water and allow them to stand for 2 minutes until soft. Stack the wrappers in a bamboo steamer and place it over a pan of boiling water. Cover the steamer and turn off the heat. This should keep the wrappers moist.*

4 *To serve, slice the duck breasts and arrange the slices on a serving platter. Serve the steamed rice paper wrappers and vegetables on another platter and pour the sauce into a jug. Let your children build their own Peking rolls.*

- 419 kcals ● 33.2 g carbohydrate
- 11 g protein ● 26 g fat ● 5.7 g fibre

50 g (2 oz) dark green cabbage,
   finely shredded
50 g (2 oz) carrot, grated
50 g (2 oz) frozen sweetcorn
about 4 tablespoons vegetable stock
150 g (5 oz) mashed potato
1 tablespoon powdered spirulina
2 tablespoons raw wheatgerm
1 tablespoon freshly grated Parmesan
   cheese
1 egg, beaten with 1 teaspoon milk or
   milk substitute
3 tablespoons wholemeal flour, or other
   suitable flour for dietary needs
2–3 tablespoons extra virgin olive oil,
   for frying

A neat idea

You can freeze the potato cakes after Step
2. Put them on a baking sheet lined with
clingfilm and place in the freezer. When
they are hard, transfer them to a freezer
bag. They can be stored for 4 weeks. To
cook them, defrost for 1–2 hours at room
temperature, brush with a little more egg,
dredge in flour and follow Step 3.

Variation

If you want to make salmon fishcakes,
replace the cooked vegetables and
spirulina with 150 g (5 oz) drained canned
salmon, and maybe add a little grated
lemon rind and a few chopped capers.

Potato
Cakes

The calming qualities of this recipe are
many; the carbohydrate in the potato has a
soporific effect on the system, the dark green
cabbage contains calcium and the sweetcorn
and wheatgerm are good sources of
magnesium. Both these minerals are
renowned for their calming qualities. The
spirulina? Well, that's just a sneaky way of
incorporating a complete vegetable protein
and some extra vitamin B12 into the diet.
Serves 2

1 *Put the cabbage, carrot and
sweetcorn into a heavy-based saucepan with
the vegetable stock and heat gently for 4–5
minutes to soften. Drain any excess liquid.*

2 *In a bowl, mix the potato, softened
vegetables, spirulina, wheatgerm, Parmesan
and half the beaten egg mixture. Using your
hands, form the mixture into 4 large patties.
Brush the potato cakes with the remaining egg
mixture and then dredge with the flour. Put
them on to a plate and allow to chill for
15–20 minutes.*

3 *Heat the oil in a frying pan and fry the
potato cakes for about 1–2 minutes on each
side, until golden brown. Drain on kitchen
paper and serve. These potato cakes are great
served with a simply grilled salmon steak and a
mixed salad, to create a totally balanced meal.*

Becadillo's Carob & Nut Brownies

If your child has a tendency to hyperactivity, but also has a sweet tooth, you can indulge them occasionally. These brownies are ideal as they contain honey, which is a natural sweetener, and caffeine-free carob instead of the usual chocolate. If your child doesn't like nuts, then replace them with an equal amount of chopped, pitted prunes or dates. **Makes 12**

1 *Cream the butter in a large mixing bowl, then add the honey, vanilla and egg and beat until you have a creamy consistency.*

2 *Mix in all the other ingredients and combine well.*

3 *Spoon the mixture into a lightly greased 18 cm (7 inch) non-stick baking tin, and smooth the top with a palette knife. Bake in a preheated oven, 350°F (180°C), Gas Mark 4, for 25–30 minutes. The mixture will puff up at first then drop to form a crust. Test it with a sharp knife or a skewer; when it is not too runny inside, it is done.*

4 *Leave the cake to cool for 5 minutes in the tin, then cut it into bars and leave to cool completely on a wire rack.*

● 237 kcals ● 21.5 g carbohydrate
● 3.8 g protein ● 16 g fat ● 1 g fibre

125 g (4 oz) butter
5 tablespoons clear honey
1½ teaspoons vanilla extract
2 eggs, lightly beaten
125 g (4 oz) wholemeal self-raising flour
2 teaspoons carob powder
125 g (4 oz) carob bar, broken into small pieces
50 g (2 oz) chopped walnuts, hazelnuts or pistachios

A neat idea

To freeze the brownies, place them in a container in layers separated by freezer paper or wrapped in foil. Defrost at room temperature for 1 hour. Reheat them at 200°C (400°F), Gas Mark 6, for 10 minutes, if liked. Can be frozen for up to 4 months.

Foods for
BRAIN POWER

Wholemeal Muffins
with Flaxseed-Enriched
Scrambled Eggs

This is a great breakfast, snack or light supper. For an added brain boost serve with strips of smoked salmon. The eggs and soya milk are good sources of lecithin, and the flaxseed oil gives an added kick of omega-3 essential fatty acids.
Serves 2

1 *Split the muffins and toast them on both sides. Spread them with butter and keep warm in a low oven.*

2 *Beat together the eggs, flaxseed oil and soya milk.*

3 *Pour the mixture into a non-stick saucepan and heat gently, stirring continuously with a wooden spoon. When the eggs start to look cooked (the consistency should be creamy and solid, not liquid), remove them from the heat and pile on to the hot muffins. Season with a little salt and pepper and garnish with a few snipped chives, if using.*

● 383 kcals ● 21 g carbohydrate
● 20 g protein ● 25 g fat ● 4 g fibre

2 wholemeal English muffins
butter, for spreading
4 eggs
1 tablespoon flaxseed oil
2 tablespoons soya milk
salt and pepper (optional)
snipped chives, to serve (optional)

A neat idea

Muffins can be frozen on the day of purchase and make a good standby ingredient, ready for use in a quick meal.

Savoury Seed *Snacks*

This snack is an excellent source of essential fatty acids and vitamin E. It can be stored for up to 2 weeks in an airtight container.

1 *Put the seeds into a bowl, add the tamari sauce and stir until all the seeds are covered with the sauce.*

2 *Heat a heavy-based frying pan until very hot.*

3 *Drain the seeds through a fine sieve, then toss them into the pan and dry-fry for a few minutes until golden brown. Remove the pan from the heat, lift out the seeds on to a piece of kitchen paper and allow to cool.*

- 1,472 kcals ● 10.3 g carbohydrate
- 67 g protein ● 125 g fat ● 20 g fibre

250 g (8 oz) assorted seeds, including
   sunflower, pumpkin, hemp, linseed and
   sesame seeds
2 tablespoons tamari sauce

Some neat ideas

These delicious crunchy seeds are also delicious sprinkled over salads, stir-fries and steamed vegetables.

Pasta
with
Nutty Salad

Pasta: ● 567 kcals ● 75 g carbohydrate
● 27 g protein ● 22.5 g fat ● 6 g fibre
Nutty Salad: ● 141 kcals
● 3.7 g carbohydrate ● 6.7 g protein
● 10.5 g fat ● 6.7 g fibre

200 g (7 oz) can tuna in olive oil
3 tablespoons pine nuts
3 tablespoons freshly grated Parmesan cheese
3 tablespoons extra virgin olive oil
325 g (11 oz) dried tagliatelle
200 g (7 oz) frozen sweetcorn
pepper (optional) and salt

Nutty Salad
200 g (7 oz) mangetout, finely sliced
200 g (7 oz) cucumber, finely sliced
2 hard-boiled eggs, quartered
25 g (1 oz) walnuts, finely chopped
1 tablespoon walnut oil
squeeze of lemon juice

To serve
finely chopped parsley
snipped chives (optional)

A neat idea

If your child doesn't like nuts, try adding a
few toasted pumpkin or sunflower seeds to
the salad, or even a sprinkle of wheatgerm.

Plenty of omega-3 fatty acids here in the
tuna, pine nuts and the olive oil, which is also
a great source of lecithin – the brain food.
The eggs and walnuts in the salad also
provide lecithin and manganese.
Serves 3–4 hungry kids

1 *Put the tuna and its oil into a food
processor or blender with the pine nuts,
Parmesan and pepper to taste, if using. Whiz to
a purée while gradually adding the olive oil.*

2 *Put the pasta into a large saucepan of
lightly salted boiling water and cook according
to packet instructions. About 2 minutes before
the pasta is al dente, add the sweetcorn.*

3 *While the pasta is cooking, make the
salad. Put the mangetout, cucumber, eggs and
walnuts into a bowl. Just before serving, add
the walnut oil and lemon juice and toss.*

4 *When the pasta and corn are cooked,
add a cupful of the pasta water to the tuna
sauce. Blend until smooth.*

5 *Drain the pasta and corn, turn into a
warm bowl and pour the sauce over. Sprinkle
with the herbs, if using, and serve immediately.*

Foods for
GROWTH

Pasta & Bean
Soup

This hearty soup is very good, and tastes even better if you make it a day in advance. It is a good source of carbohydrates and protein. Omit the bacon (and cheese) to make a vegetarian (or vegan) alternative.
Serves 4

1 *Put the beans into a saucepan and cover them with cold water. Bring to the boil and boil for 2 minutes, then remove the pan from the heat and leave to stand for 2 hours.*

2 *Heat the oil in a frying pan, add the onion, garlic and bacon, if using, and cook until the onion has softened.*

3 *Drain the beans thoroughly and transfer them to a large saucepan. Add the onion and bacon mixture, pour in the stock and stir in the tomato purée. Bring to the boil, then pour the soup into a casserole dish.*

4 *Transfer the covered casserole to a preheated oven, 180°C (350°F), Gas Mark 4, and cook for about 3 hours. Remove the casserole*

from the oven and purée half the soup in a food processor or blender.

5 *Stir the puréed soup back into the casserole, add the macaroni, parsley and basil and cook for another 45 minutes. Serve with a little grated Cheddar or Parmesan cheese, a side salad and some crusty wholemeal bread.*

● 437 kcals ● 40 g carbohydrate
● 13 g protein ● 25 g fat ● 5.5 g fibre

250 g (8 oz) dried haricot beans
2 tablespoons vegetable oil
1 large onion, chopped
2 garlic cloves, crushed
125 g (4 oz) bacon, finely chopped (optional)
600 ml (1 pint) vegetable stock
3 tablespoons tomato purée
125 g (4 oz) short-cut macaroni
2 tablespoons finely chopped parsley
1 teaspoon finely chopped basil
Cheddar or Parmesan cheese, to serve

Fish
in a
Jacket

I don't believe there's a child who doesn't like potatoes baked in their jackets. Tuna and sweetcorn are as popular a potato filling as baked beans and cheese. Growth-promoting protein is supplied by the cheese and the tuna, and the latter is also a great source of essential fatty acids, vitamin B complex, vitamin D, selenium, iron, zinc and sulphur. The potatoes are full of energy-giving carbohydrates.

Serves 4

1 *Pierce the potatoes all over with a fork. Place them on a rack in a preheated oven, 200°C (400°F), Gas Mark 6, and bake for 1 hour. Leave the oven on.*

2 *Cut the potatoes in half lengthways, scoop the flesh into a bowl and mash it with the tuna, mayonnaise, celery, sweetcorn and parsley.*

3 *Arrange the potato skins on a baking sheet. Spoon the filling into the skins then sprinkle with grated Cheddar. Return to the oven for 15 minutes. For a balanced meal, serve with a side salad of lettuce, tomatoes, grated carrot and avocado.*

- 422 kcals ● 24 g carbohydrate
- 19 g protein ● 27 g fat ● 5 g fibre

4 baking potatoes
175 g (6 oz) canned tuna in oil, drained
100 ml (3 fl oz) mayonnaise
1 celery stick, finely chopped
50 g (2 oz) frozen sweetcorn
1 tablespoon finely chopped parsley
50 g (2 oz) Cheddar cheese, grated

A neat idea

If you like, you could substitute haddock, salmon or mackerel for the tuna. If you are cooking for vegetarians, try 175 g (6 oz) silken tofu in place of the fish.

Falafel

The beauty of this vegetarian dish is that the combination of chickpeas and bulgar wheat provides a complete protein, and it is full of vitamin B1 and folic acid. Serve the falafel warm with wholemeal pitta bread, a large green salad and some Greek yogurt for an extra source of all-important calcium.
Makes 12–16

1 *Soak the chickpeas overnight in a bowl with plenty of cold water.*

2 *Drain the chickpeas, place them in a saucepan and cover with plenty of fresh water. Bring to the boil and boil for 10 minutes. Reduce the heat and simmer for 1–1½ hours until the chickpeas are soft. Drain.*

3 *Meanwhile, soak the bulgar wheat in warm water for 1 hour. Drain.*

4 *Put the chickpeas, bulgar wheat, onion, garlic, parsley, cumin, coriander and baking powder in a food processor or blender. Season to taste, if you like, and process until the mixture forms a firm paste. Shape into walnut-sized balls and flatten slightly.*

5 *Put the oil into a deep heavy-based frying pan and heat it until a small piece of the falafel mixture sizzles. Fry the falafels in batches until golden. Drain on kitchen paper and allow to cool slightly before serving.*

- 195 kcals ● 12 g carbohydrate
- 5 g protein ● 15 g fat ● 3 g fibre

125 g (4 oz) dried chickpeas
25 g (1 oz) bulgar wheat
1 large onion, roughly chopped
2 garlic cloves, roughly chopped
4 tablespoons chopped parsley
1 teaspoon cumin seeds, crushed
1 teaspoon coriander seeds, crushed
½ teaspoon baking powder
salt and pepper (optional)
4 tablespoons extra virgin olive oil

A neat idea

The falafels can be frozen after Step 4. Put them on a baking sheet lined with clingfilm and freeze for 30 minutes until hard, then transfer to a freezer bag. They can be stored for up to 4 weeks. To cook, defrost at room temperature for 1–2 hours and fry as described in Step 5.

Foods to boost the immune SYSTEM

Carrot
&
Tomato Soup

This warming soup gives a great boost to the immune system as it is full of beta-carotene and vitamins A and C.
Serves 4

1 *Heat the oil in a saucepan and sauté the onion, garlic, red pepper and thyme for 3–5 minutes until soft. Add the carrots and potato and continue cooking for a few minutes.*

2 *Stir in the stock and tomatoes and bring to the boil. Reduce the heat, cover the saucepan and simmer for 20 minutes.*

3 *Pour the soup into a food processor or blender and purée until smooth. Return the soup to the pan, add the soya milk, season with salt and pepper if wished, then heat the soup until it is hot but not boiling. Serve garnished with grated carrot, a sprinkling of parsley and a spoonful of Greek yogurt or soured cream.*

- 178 kcals ● 20.7 g carbohydrate
- 5.2 g protein ● 9.75 g fat
- 6.4 g fibre

2 tablespoons extra virgin olive oil
1 onion, chopped
3 garlic cloves, chopped
1 red pepper, cored, deseeded and chopped
1 teaspoon chopped thyme
3 carrots, thinly sliced
1 potato, diced
500 ml (17 fl oz) vegetable stock
125 g (4 oz) fresh or canned tomatoes
250 ml (8 fl oz) soya milk
salt and pepper (optional)

A neat idea

Allow the soup to cool after it is puréed and freeze in a microwavable container. If storage is limited in the freezer, halve the amount of liquid used. Defrost in the microwave or at room temperature. Add the remaining liquid, if necessary, and reheat in the microwave or over a pan of boiling water, adding the soya milk and seasoning. Will freeze for up to six months.

Tomato, Garlic &
Herb Loaf

This loaf is an excellent way to pack in some immune-boosting garlic, and it is healthier than the usual garlic bread, because it uses unsaturated olive oil instead of butter. Tomatoes are a good source of the phytonutrient lycopene, which is a powerful antioxidant.
Serves 4–8

1 *Make deep diagonal cuts in the French stick every 4 cm (1½ inches), cutting almost but not quite through the loaf.*

2 *In a bowl, mix together the olive oil, tomato purée, garlic and parsley.*

3 *Fill each cut in the loaf with a generous spoonful of the garlic mixture, being careful to ensure that both sides are evenly coated. Wrap the loaf in foil and bake in a preheated oven, 180°C (350°F) Gas Mark 4, for 20–25 minutes.*

1 small wholewheat or white wholegrain French stick
3 tablespoons extra virgin olive oil
2 tablespoons tomato purée
3 garlic cloves, crushed
2 tablespoons finely chopped parsley

Some neat ideas

The loaf can be wrapped in foil and frozen at the pre-baking stage. Defrost at room temperature for 1 hour and cook as described in Step 3. Will freeze for up to six months.

For children with a gluten allergy, try the tomato mixture on jacket potatoes or spread it generously over oat or rice flour pancakes – or use gluten-free bread.

This garlic filling also works well spread on wholemeal pitta bread and placed under a hot grill for a few minutes.

Per slice: ● 108 kcals
● 12.6 g carbohydrate ● 2.4 g protein
● 5.6 g fat ● 1 g fibre

- ● 663 kcals ● 115 g carbohydrate
- ● 14.9 g protein ● 18.6 g fat
- ● 14.2 g fibre

4 tablespoons vegetable oil
1 large onion, finely chopped
3 garlic cloves, finely chopped
375 g (12 oz) brown rice
1 litre (1¾ pints) hot vegetable stock
500 g (1 lb) tomatoes, skinned and chopped
250 g (8 oz) broccoli, chopped
500 g (1 lb) frozen sweetcorn
3–4 tablespoons finely chopped coriander
salt and pepper or vegetable bouillon
    powder

A neat idea

You could ring the changes by replacing
the frozen sweetcorn with baby corn and
the broccoli with mangetout, if liked.

Broccoli, Tomato & Corn
Risotto

This risotto is made with brown rice instead
of the traditional arborio, so not only is it
healthier, but also you won't have to spend
so long ritualistically stirring in the stock. It is
a splendid immune booster as broccoli and
tomatoes are both major antioxidants.
Serves 4

1 *Heat the oil in a large saucepan and
lightly sauté the onion and garlic until soft and
lightly browned.*

2 *Add the rice and cook for 1–2 minutes,
stirring constantly, until the grains are golden.*

3 *Add the hot stock, the tomatoes and
the broccoli and stir to combine. Cover the pan
and simmer for about 25 minutes.*

4 *When the rice is nearly done, add the
sweetcorn and coriander and cook for a further
5 minutes, or until the rice is al dente.*

5 *Stir the risotto and season with salt
and pepper or vegetable bouillon powder.
Serve immediately.*

Winter
WARMERS

Power Pancakes
with Fruit Purée

- 222 kcals ● 27.7 g carbohydrate
- 13.45 g protein ● 5.75 g fat
- 6.7 g fibre

50 g (2 oz) rolled oats
1 egg
75 g (3 oz) cottage cheese
¼ teaspoon natural vanilla extract
1 teaspoon peanut or almond butter
vegetable oil, for greasing

Fruit Purée
200 g (7 oz) strawberries
50 ml (2 fl oz) apple juice

To serve
50 g (2 oz) strawberries and raspberries
2 tablespoons live yogurt (optional)
1 tablespoon chopped nuts (optional)

When the cold weather sets in, these pancakes make a good, healthy, hot breakfast, or you could serve them at teatime. They are quick and easy to make – you could even make the batter the night before and refrigerate it overnight. Drizzle the pancakes with fruit purée for a vitamin-fortified start to the day.
Serves 2

1 *Put the rolled oats into a food processor or blender and process on high for 1 minute to make flour. Turn into a bowl and add the egg, cottage cheese, vanilla extract and peanut or almond butter. Stir until mixed.*

2 *To make the fruit purée, whiz the fruit and apple juice together in a food processor.*

3 *Add spoonfuls of the batter mixture to a hot, lightly greased griddle or heavy-based frying pan. Cook the pancakes for a few minutes on both sides, re-oiling the griddle or frying pan for each one as necessary.*

A neat idea

For the fruit purée you can use any fruit available in season, for example mango, papaya, blueberries, blackberries or kiwifruit.

4 *To serve, pour the fruit purée over the pancakes, scatter with the fresh fruit and add a dollop of live yogurt and a sprinkling of chopped nuts, if liked.*

Chicken Soup
with Barley

This soup provides such a boost when you are unwell – the onions, garlic and carrots are excellent at fighting infections, and the chicken is a healthy source of protein that helps maintain the body when you are ill. **Serves 8**

- ●290 kcals ●13.9 g carbohydrate
- ● 42.9 g protein ● 6.2 g fat
- ● 2.9 g fibre

1 large chicken, weighing about 2.5 kg (5 lb), cut into quarters
3 onions
3 large carrots
3 celery sticks
6 garlic cloves
4 bay leaves
50 g (2 oz) pearl barley
2 chicken stock cubes
4 tablespoons chopped parsley
salt and pepper (optional)

1 *Place the chicken in a large saucepan with 1 quartered onion, 1 quartered carrot, 1 quartered celery stick, the garlic cloves and bay leaves. Cover with water and bring to the boil. Cover the pan and simmer for 1–1½ hours, until the meat pulls away from the bones.*

2 *Lift the chicken pieces out with a slotted spoon and allow to cool. Remove the carrot, celery, onion and garlic and reserve.*

3 *Chop the chicken into bite-sized pieces and set aside. Reserve the bones.*

4 *Skim any fat from the surface of the stock. Put the chicken bones back into the saucepan and add about 500 ml (1 pint) water. Bring to the boil, then reduce the heat and simmer for 1 hour.*

5 *Strain the stock through a sieve and return the liquid to the saucepan. Put the reserved carrot, celery, onion and garlic cloves into a food processor or blender and add*

1 ladleful of strained stock. Purée until smooth then stir into the remaining stock.

6 *Finely chop the remaining carrots, onions and celery and add them to the stock. Add the pearl barley and crumble in the stock cubes for extra flavour. Cook until the pearl barley and vegetables are tender. Add the chicken and the parsley. Season to taste, if liked, and serve.*

Coconut & Citrus
Rice Pudding

- 385 kcals ● 34 g carbohydrate
- 5.9 g protein ● 27.5 g fat
- 1.9 g fibre

This is a very tasty twist on an old favourite. Even though the coconut milk contains saturated fat, it is very high in calcium, magnesium, phosphorus and zinc, which play an important role in the immune system. Your children will love the tangy orange flavour and benefit from the extra vitamin C. **Serves 4**

1 *Using half the melted butter, grease a 1 litre (1¾ pint) ovenproof dish.*

2 *Put the milk, coconut milk, orange juice, vanilla extract and honey into a saucepan and warm through gently, until the honey has melted.*

3 *Put the rice into the greased dish and pour over the milk mixture. Sprinkle with the orange rind and pour the remaining melted butter over the top. Place in a preheated oven, 150°C (300°F), Gas Mark 2, and bake for 2½ hours, stirring after the first 30 minutes, and again 30 minutes later. Serve with a drizzle of honey and a dollop of Greek yogurt.*

50 g (2 oz) butter, melted
200 ml (7 fl oz) skimmed or soya milk
400 ml (14 fl oz) can coconut milk
juice and rind of 1 orange
½ teaspoon natural vanilla extract
2 tablespoons honey
75 g (3 oz) pudding rice

A neat idea

If you wish to freeze this dish cook it in a foil-lined casserole dish. Allow to cool and freeze. Once frozen, remove from the dish and wrap in the foil. Defrost partially while still wrapped in foil, then place in a casserole dish and bake at 200°C (400°F), Gas Mark 6 for 30 minutes. Can be frozen for up to four months.

- 384 kcals ● 36.6 g carbohydrate
- 11.7 g protein ● 22.9 g fat
- 3.2 g fibre

750 g (1½ lb) potatoes, grated
4 tablespoons extra virgin olive oil
4 tablespoons tomato purée
1 garlic clove, crushed
selection of toppings such as sliced
   mushrooms, sliced tomatoes, sweetcorn,
   finely sliced spring onion, olives, capers,
   finely chopped red and green peppers
   (cooked turkey or chicken or prawns for
   non-vegetarians)
175 g (6 oz) goats' cheese, crumbled
   (or grated Cheddar)
2 teaspoons chopped oregano
salt and pepper (optional)

A neat idea

Vegans could use soya cheese instead of
goats' cheese or Cheddar.

Potato
Pizza

The key here is the wheat-free pizza base.
You can vary the toppings as you like. The
nutritional analysis per serving is based on
the ingredients shown in the photograph.
Serves 4

1 *Squeeze the grated potato in kitchen paper to remove any excess liquid.*

2 *Heat 1 tablespoon of oil in a heavy-based frying pan. Add a quarter of the potato and flatten it to a round just smaller than the pan. Cook for 4–5 minutes on each side until the base is crisp and golden. Place on a baking sheet and repeat with the remaining potato.*

3 *Mix the tomato purée and garlic and spread evenly over the bases, out to the edges.*

4 *Get everybody to choose toppings and build their pizzas. Finish with cheese, oregano, and salt and pepper, if liked.*

5 *Place the pizzas under a preheated hot grill for about 5–10 minutes, until the toppings have cooked and the cheese has melted.*

Fragrant Thai Fried
Noodles

This Thai dish is based on rice noodles, fresh herbs and finely shredded raw vegetables. I have adapted it for children's taste buds by replacing the usual pork or prawns with lean turkey, which is a great, cheap and healthy option. I have omitted the chillies, although you could add a small one if you have older children who enjoy a bit of hot spice. Ingredients such as Thai fish sauce and rice noodles are usually available in large supermarkets but if not, look in your phone book for your nearest oriental supplier. This is a dish that takes time to prepare but minutes to cook, so get the kids to help.
Serves 4

1 *Soak the dried rice noodles in warm water for 10 minutes, or until they are soft. Drain and set aside.*

2 *Heat the oil in a wok or large frying pan. When it is very hot, add the garlic and turkey and toss and stir for 5 minutes.*

3 *Add the chives and the noodles, cover the pan and cook for 1 more minute. Add the fish sauce, lime juice, honey and eggs to the wok and toss well with tongs or 2 wooden spoons until heated through.*

● **537 kcals** ● **66 g carbohydrate**
● **26.5 g protein** ● **18.6 g fat**
● **6.37 g fibre**

250 g (8 oz) dried rice noodles
2 tablespoons extra virgin olive oil
3 garlic cloves, finely chopped
250 g (8 oz) lean turkey breast, finely sliced
50 g (2 oz) chives, finely chopped
2 tablespoons Thai fish sauce
2 tablespoons lime juice
1 tablespoon honey
2 eggs, beaten
75 g (3 oz) bean sprouts
coriander sprigs, finely chopped
a few basil leaves, finely chopped
50 g (2 oz) unsalted peanuts or cashews,
   finely chopped
75 g (3 oz) carrot, coarsely grated
75 g (3 oz) cucumber, cut into fine julienne strips

A neat idea

Experiment with various combinations of finely shredded raw vegetables. Options include yellow or red peppers and courgettes.

4 *Add the bean sprouts and toss until heated through.*

5 *Transfer the contents of the wok to a heated serving platter and sprinkle over the coriander, basil, nuts, carrot and cucumber. Serve immediately.*

2 ripe bananas – to make 250 g (8 oz)
    when mashed
2 egg whites, lightly beaten
150 g (5 oz) dates, pitted and chopped
140 g (4½ oz) oats
75 g (3 oz) raisins

Some neat ideas

Replace the wheat flour in baking recipes
with a mixture of rice flour, millet flour
and ground porridge oats, using one third
of each.

To freeze, once the cookies are cool, place
them in a container with freezer paper
between the layers. Leave in wrapping to
defrost. Will freeze for up to six months.

Oat & Fruit
Cookies

These naturally sweet, chewy cookies taste
far better than any shop-bought alternative.
They are virtually fat-free and packed with
energy for your children.
Makes 16

1 *Roughly mash the bananas, leaving
some chunks. Add the egg whites and dates
and mix thoroughly. Stir in the oats and raisins.
Set aside for 10 minutes.*

2 *Place teaspoons of the dough on
lightly greased baking sheets and flatten with
a spoon. Bake in a preheated oven, 180°C
(350°F), Gas Mark 4, for 20–25 minutes until
the edges are lightly browned.*

3 *Remove the baking sheets from the
oven and leave the cookies to cool, then
remove to a wire rack. The cookies can be
stored in an airtight container in the
refrigerator for up to 4 days.*

● 47.5 kcals ● 9 g carbohydrate
● 0.8 g protein ● 0.9 g fat
● 0.9 g fibre

Foods for the
SICK CHILD

Asparagus
with Garlic Dressing

This recipe may sound a little indulgent, but it makes good finger food for a poorly child who needs a bit of culinary stimulation, and it is incredibly quick to make. Asparagus is a good mild vegetable that encourages elimination of toxins, and the garlic and oregano are antibacterial and antiviral.

Serves 4

1 *Put the oil, mustard, lemon juice, vinegar, garlic, honey and oregano into a food processor or blender and blend for 30 seconds.*

2 *Snap off the ends of the asparagus and put the spears into a pan with a little water and a sprinkling of vegetable bouillon powder. Bring the water to the boil, then cover the pan and cook for 2–3 minutes or until just done.*

3 *Drain the asparagus and serve, warm or cold, tossed in the garlic dressing.*

- 306 kcals ● 10.1 g carbohydrate
- 6.9 g protein ● 26.6 g fat
- 2.8 g fibre

150 ml (¼ pint) extra virgin olive oil
½ teaspoon Dijon mustard
2 tablespoons lemon juice
2 tablespoons cider vinegar
2 garlic cloves, crushed
2 teaspoons honey
1 tablespoon finely chopped oregano
750 g (1½ lb) fresh asparagus, preferably the tiny spears rather than the thick plump ones
vegetable bouillon powder, to taste
salt and pepper (optional)

A neat idea

Try creamy hummus with plenty of garlic as an alternative dip.

Sweet & Sour
Salad

This is a truly delicious recipe – very healthy and full of nutrients. It is just throbbing with beta-carotene, vitamin C and zinc, and there are the antiseptic qualities of the limes and tomatoes, and of course the soothing papaya. It is perfect for sore little throats and chesty coughs.
Serves 2–3

1 *In a large salad bowl, combine the avocado, mango, papaya, peeled prawns and cherry tomatoes.*

2 *Drizzle with the oil and lime juice, add a little salt and pepper, if using, then toss and sprinkle with the chives. Serve with wholemeal bread, if liked.*

1 avocado, peeled and cubed
1 mango, peeled and cubed
1 papaya, peeled, deseeded and cubed
175 g (6 oz) cooked peeled prawns
200 g (7 oz) cherry tomatoes, halved
2 tablespoons olive or flaxseed oil
juice of 1 lime
handful of snipped chives
salt and pepper (optional)

A neat idea

This salad tastes just as good without the prawns, so leave them out if you are feeding vegetarians, vegans or anybody allergic to shellfish. Prawns should never be given to a child under two years of age.

- 355 kcals ● 24 g carbohydrate
- 14 g protein ● 22 g fat
- 4.4 g fibre

Fresh Fruit
Lollies

These fresh juice lollies are a good way of giving your child a vitamin boost, and they will soothe even the sorest of throats.
Makes 4

1 *Juice the fruit, alternating the pineapple with the blackcurrants to ensure that the juice flows freely.*

2 *Pour the juice into four small lolly moulds and freeze immediately, before all the goodness has had a chance to slip away.*

● 40 kcals ● 9.3 g carbohydrate
● 0.7 g protein ● trace fat
● trace fibre

375 g (12 oz) pineapple, chopped
375 g (12 oz) blackcurrants, fresh or frozen

Some neat ideas

Try any of these combinations of vitamin C-packed juices: 4 oranges and 2 peaches; 200 g (7 oz) watermelon and 200 g (7 oz) strawberries; ½ papaya, 1 orange and 150 g (5 oz) raspberries; 3 apples and 200 g (7 oz) blackberries.

For colds, flu and sore throats, increase levels of zinc and vitamin C and give a spoonful of natural honey to ease the sore throat.

These lollies can be frozen for up two months. Eat them from frozen.

- 185 kcals ● 38 g carbohydrate
- 7 g protein ● 1.6 g fat
- 7 g fibre

100 g (3½ oz) brown rice, rinsed
100 g (3½ oz) pearl barley, rinsed
600 ml (1 pint) vegetable stock
125 g (4 oz) canned kidney beans, rinsed
   and drained
100 g (3½ oz) frozen peas
2 carrots, grated
handful of parsley, finely chopped
salt and pepper (optional)

Some neat ideas

When your child is fully recovered, this dish can be eaten cold with a sprinkling of pumpkin seeds and a dressing of flaxseed or olive oil with lemon juice, or make it a regular addition to the diet of a child who is prone to constipation.

For a bit of variety, add sweetcorn, chopped courgettes and red peppers. If your child likes herbs and spices, add chopped coriander leaves and a pinch of ground cumin, while a few raisins, pine nuts and some grated orange rind will give a North African flavour. Chopped tomatoes and spring onions would also work well with some fresh basil.

Absolutely Not
Fried Rice

Rice is very gentle on the stomach and is good for diarrhoea. Kidney beans cleanse the digestive tract, while barley soothes it. Carrots are antibacterial and antiviral and, along with the parsley, stimulate and purify liver and kidney function.
Serves 2–3

1 *Put the rice, barley and stock into a large pan and bring to the boil. Turn down the heat, cover the pan and simmer for about 20 minutes until the rice and barley are cooked.*

2 *Drain the rice and barley, return them to the pan and add the kidney beans. Cover the pan with a clean tea towel and the lid, and set aside. The tea towel will absorb moisture and keep the grains separate.*

3 *Cook the peas in boiling water for 3–4 minutes. Drain and add to the rice mixture.*

4 *Stir the carrots and parsley into the rice and season, if liked. Serve the rice on its own, or with some poached chicken, if your child's tummy is still a little sensitive.*

Pear & Apple
Juice

- 250 kcals ● 63 g carbohydrate
- 2 g protein ● 0.6 g fat
- trace fibre

2 pears, sliced
2 apples, sliced
ice cubes

Apart from being a brilliant vitamin-enriched tonic, this juice is an excellent natural laxative. For added potency, stir in a couple of tablespoons of prune juice.
Serves 1

1 *Juice the pears and apples, then put them into a food processor or blender with a couple of ice cubes. Blend briefly and pour into a tall glass. Serve immediately.*

A neat idea

Pour into ice lolly containers or ice cube containers and, once frozen, transfer to freezer bags. Either eat frozen, as lollies, or whiz the cubes in a blender with other fruit to give an added boost to fruit smoothies. Will freeze for up to 2 months.

Blueberry
Slush

Blueberries are very good if your child has had a stomach upset as they contain anthocyanosides, which are lethal to the bacteria that can cause the problem. As fruit may aggravate diarrhoea, it is better to give this drink to your child when their stomach is starting to settle, as a clean-up operation, along with plenty of live yogurt to normalize the intestinal flora. This is a little like a sorbet, and very mild-tasting. So, if your child is still feeling poorly, it should go down very well.
Serves 2

1 *Put the blueberries through a juicer. This may not produce much juice, but it is the residual pulp that you need. Scrape the pulp into a bowl and stir in any juice that you may have extracted.*

2 *Transfer to a freezer container and freeze for 1 hour.*

3 *Remove the blueberry slush from the freezer and allow it to soften slightly before eating.*

- 63.5 kcals ● 12.5 g carbohydrate
- 2.2 g protein ● 0.5 g fat
- 16.8 g fibre

500 g (1 lb) fresh or frozen blueberries

A neat idea

Can be frozen for up to 2 months. Defrost slightly before eating.

Foods to treat
COLDS & FLU

Cod Parcels
with
Hot Millet Tabbouleh

These cod parcels are very light and easy to digest, and the lemon and ginger will help clear excess mucus. The onions and garlic in the tabbouleh are antiviral and antibacterial and, together with the parsley, they act as a decongestant. The lemon and tomatoes are powerful antioxidants and full of vitamin C.
Serves 2

1 Place each cod fillet on a piece of greaseproof paper, large enough to wrap it up. Sprinkle each fillet with 1 teaspoon of the lemon juice, a little oil, a little garlic and ½ teaspoon of the chopped ginger. Fold and seal the edges of the greaseproof paper to form airtight parcels, being careful to allow some space above the fish.

2 Arrange the parcels on a baking tray with a little cold water in the bottom and bake in a preheated oven, 180°C (350°F), Gas Mark 4,

for 20 minutes, or until the cod is firm to the touch. It will literally steam in its own juices.

3 Put the millet into a small saucepan with about 175 ml (6 fl oz) cold water and the bouillon powder. Bring to the boil and simmer for 20 minutes, or until the millet is cooked.

4 Meanwhile, make the dressing. Put the remaining lemon juice, oil and garlic in a food processor or blender with the tomatoes, spring onion and honey and blend until smooth.

5 Drain the millet and put it into a bowl. Add the dressing and parsley and mix well. Serve immediately with the cod fillets.

- 352 kcals ● 44 g carbohydrate
- 11.9 g protein ● 14.8 g fat
- 2.9 g fibre

2 cod fillets, skinned
juice of 2 lemons
2 tablespoons extra virgin olive oil
2 garlic cloves, finely chopped
1 teaspoon finely chopped fresh root ginger
75 g (3 oz) millet
1 teaspoon vegetable bouillon powder
2 tomatoes, skinned, deseeded and chopped
1 spring onion, chopped
1 teaspoon honey
1 tablespoon chopped parsley

Chicken Noodle Soup
with Heart and Star Croûtons

This recipe is simple to make and easy to digest. The broth is light and the garlic and ginger combination is excellent to help shift mucus from the respiratory tract.
Serves 2–3

1 *Put the stock into a saucepan with the carrot, onion, garlic, bay leaf, cloves and ginger. Bring to the boil, cover the pan and simmer for 30 minutes.*

2 *Strain the stock and discard the vegetables and spices. Return the liquid to the pan and add the vermicelli. Bring to the boil and simmer for 10 minutes, until the vermicelli is cooked.*

3 *Toast the bread on both sides, then make croûtons using star- and heart-shaped cutters. Stir the chopped parsley into the soup and serve in bowls, decorated with the shaped croûtons.*

● 118 kcals ● 23 g carbohydrate
● 4.2 g protein ● 0.8 g fat
● 4 g fibre

600 ml (1 pint) fresh chicken or
    vegetable stock
1 carrot, chopped
1 onion, chopped
2 garlic cloves, chopped
1 bay leaf
2 cloves
2.5 cm (1 inch) cube fresh root ginger,
    finely chopped
50 g (2 oz) vermicelli, broken into
    small pieces
2 slices wholemeal bread
1 tablespoon finely chopped parsley
salt and pepper (optional)

Some neat ideas

If your children are allergic to wheat or gluten, replace the vermicelli with extra fine rice noodles.

Chicken Soup with Barley (page 120); Carrot & Tomato Soup (page 114) and Leek & Potato Soup (page 98) are also good for colds, flu and bacterial infections.

To freeze, allow the soup to cool, then put in a casserole dish or wide-mouthed freezer container. Either defrost in the microwave, or at room temperature for 2–3 hours. Reheat in the microwave or over a pan of boiling water. Will freeze for up to six months.

Citrus
Juice

This juice is full of vitamins A and C, which should help kick your child's cold into touch. Citrus fruits are great mucus reducers.
Serves 1

1 *Juice the carrot and the oranges and serve immediately.*

- 188 kcals ● 35 g carbohydrate
- 5 g protein ● 0.8 g fat
- trace fibre

1 carrot, weighing about 125 g (4 oz)
2 oranges, weighing about 200 g (7 oz), segmented

A neat idea

Making your own juice allows you plenty of scope to experiment with flavours. Vary this recipe by adding apple and/or grated fresh root ginger.

Common childhood
AILMENTS

Healthy
Sweet Bread

This tasty bread is a good way to incorporate a few extra vegetables into your child's diet. It is beautifully moist and can be served with a little fruit purée (or butter) for a perfect teatime treat while recuperating.
Makes about 10–12 portions

1 *Place the bulgar wheat in a bowl and cover with boiling water. Let it stand for 30 minutes, then drain.*

2 *Beat the eggs until they are light and foamy, then add the oil, honey, vanilla, grated fruit and/or vegetables and the bulgar wheat.*

3 *Mix together the flour, cinnamon, baking soda and dried fruit and add to the egg mixture. When the mixture is well combined, pour it into an oiled 1 kg (2 lb) loaf tin or a flat rectangular baking tin. Bake in a preheated oven, 170°C (325°F), Gas Mark 3, for 40–50 minutes, or until a sharp knife or skewer comes out clean when inserted into the centre of the loaf.*

- 176 kcals ● 32.5 g carbohydrate
- 4.7 g protein ● 3.2 g fat
- 3.2 g fibre

125 g (4 oz) fine bulgar wheat
2 eggs
150 ml (5 fl oz) vegetable oil
125 g (4 oz) honey
1 teaspoon natural vanilla extract
375 g (12 oz) coarsely grated courgette, carrot, apple or squash, or any combination of the four
250 g (8 oz) wholemeal flour, sifted
1½ teaspoons ground cinnamon
2 teaspoons baking soda
125 g (4 oz) sultanas, dried apricots, sour cherries or raisins

A neat idea

To freeze, allow the loaf to cool, then wrap it in foil or freezer paper. Defrost in its wrapping at room temperature for 2–3 hours. Slice while partially frozen to prevent crumbling. Will freeze for up to four months.

- 382 kcals ● 23 g carbohydrate
- 13 g protein ● 27 g fat
- 4.5 g fibre

625 g (1¼ lb) large potatoes, chopped
65 g (2½ oz) butter
2 tablespoons olive oil
1 onion, finely chopped
1 carrot, finely chopped
1 celery stick, finely chopped
2 garlic cloves, finely chopped
250 g (8 oz) minced lamb
50 ml (2 fl oz) apple juice
200 g (7 oz) can tomatoes
1 teaspoon tamari sauce
50 g (2 oz) Cheddar cheese, grated,
   to sprinkle (optional)

Some neat ideas

For a vegetarian option replace the lamb with a mixture of bulgar wheat, puy lentils and millet to provide a complete protein alternative.

If the meat sauce is too liquid at the end of Step 3, add some soaked bulgar wheat or couscous for added bulk.

Allow the pie to cool in its cooking dish before freezing. Partially defrost, then cook at 200°C (400°F), Gas Mark 6, for 30 minutes. Sprinkle with some grated cheese 10 minutes before the end of cooking time. Will freeze for up to six months.

Cold Comfort
Shepherd's Pie

This is another winter favourite that always goes down well with children. It is full of protein, carbohydrates, vitamins and minerals.
Serves 4–6

1 *Boil the potatoes until soft, then drain and mash with a potato masher. Beat in the butter.*

2 *Heat the oil in a large frying pan and fry the onion, carrot, celery and garlic for about 10 minutes.*

3 *Add the meat and break it up with a wooden spoon. Add the apple juice, tomatoes and tamari sauce. Stir well, then cover the pan and simmer for 20 minutes. Remove the lid, stir again and simmer for a further 10 minutes.*

4 *Tip the contents of the pan into a 25 cm (10 inch) oval dish and top with the potato, starting at the outer edges of the dish and working inwards so the potato does not sink into the meat. Sprinkle with a little grated cheese, if required.*

5 *Cook the pie in a preheated oven, 190°C (375°F), Gas Mark 5, for 30 minutes or place under a hot grill for about 5 minutes. Serve with broccoli or another seasonal green vegetable.*

Vegetable Chips
with Pumpkin Dip

Nutritious and delicious, these vegetable chips are full of beta-carotene, vitamins and minerals. The beetroot contains inulin, which promotes the development of healthy bacteria, so it is particularly helpful if your child has had antibiotics. The pumpkin dip is a tasty way to give a child a boost of essential fatty acids, and all the raw ingredients will help guard against further infection, by giving the immune system a good boost.
Serves 4

1 *Cut all the vegetables into julienne strips about 1 cm (½ inch) thick.*

2 *Put the oil into a large baking tray and heat in a preheated oven, 200°C (400°F), Gas Mark 6, until hot.*

3 *Scatter the vegetable chips over the baking tray, making sure they are all covered in oil. Return the tray to the oven and cook for 20 minutes, or until the chips are lightly browned on the outside and soft on the inside. Keep checking and shaking the tray while they are cooking.*

4 *Meanwhile, make the pumpkin dip. Dry-fry the pumpkin seeds in a frying pan over*

- 534 kcals ● 50.8 g carbohydrate
- 16.4 g protein ● 32 g fat
- 12 g fibre

1 large baking potato
2 parsnips
1 sweet potato
2 carrots
250 g (8 oz) celeriac
1 large uncooked beetroot
3–4 tablespoons olive oil

Pumpkin Dip
175 g (6 oz) pumpkin seeds
2 garlic cloves, finely chopped
3–5 spring onions, chopped
½ teaspoon ground cumin
3 large tomatoes, skinned, deseeded
  and diced
juice of ½ lime
3 tablespoons tomato purée

a moderate heat for 5–10 minutes. Shake the pan and turn them as they pop and go golden brown. Remove the pan from the heat and allow to cool. Grind the seeds coarsely in a spice grinder or food processor. Add the garlic, spring onions, ground cumin, tomatoes, lime juice and tomato purée and blend until the mixture becomes quite smooth.

INDEX

Executive editor Nicola Hill
Editor Sharon Ashman
Design manager Tokiko Morishima
Designer Louise Griffiths
Picture researcher Christine
    Junemann
Senior production controller
    Jo Sim
Special photography David Jordan
Food stylist Oona van den Berg
Stylist Judy Williams

Acknowledgements

Bubbles/Frans-Rombout 92/Ian
    West 74, 78/John Powell 57/Lucy
    Tizard 53 bottom
Corbis UK Ltd/Mike Buxton 75/Paul
    A. Souders 30
**Octopus Publishing Group
    Limited** 47/Stephen Conroy 53
    top/Peter Pugh Cook front cover
    left, front cover right, back cover top
    right, back cover centre left, back
    cover bottom right, 1 centre right, 2
    top left, 3 centre, 4 top left, 5, 11,
    21, 23, 46, 49, 50 top left, 51, 56,
    62/David Jordan front cover centre,
    front cover bottom centre right, front
    cover bottom centre, back cover top
    left, back cover bottom left, back
    cover centre right, back cover centre
    right top, back cover bottom centre
    left, back cover bottom centre right,
    1 top left, 1 centre, 1 bottom left, 2
    centre left, 2 top right, 2 centre
    right, 2 bottom right, 2 bottom left,
    3 top left, 3 centre right, 3 bottom
    right, 4 centre left, 4 bottom right, 4
    bottom left, 4 bottom centre, 8, 9,
    15, 18, 20, 24, 25, 26, 27, 31, 33,
    34, 35, 36, 37, 38, 39, 40, 41, 42,
    43, 44, 45, 50 bottom right, 58,
    59, 61, 64, 65, 67, 69, 71, 72, 73,
    76, 77, 79, 80, 81, 83, 84, 85, 86,
    87, 88, 89, 93, 94, 95, 97, 99,
    101, 103, 105, 107, 108, 109,
    111, 113, 115, 117, 119, 120,
    123, 125, 127, 128, 129, 131,
    132, 133, 135, 137, 139,
    141/Sandra Lane 55/ Tessa
    Musgrave 60/Peter Myers 14 right/
    Sean Myers 54/Philip Webb 14
    left/Mark Winwood 13
**Mother and Baby Picture
    Library**/Eddie Lawrence 91
Photodisc 10, 12, 22, 29, 63
Getty Images Stone/Ken Fisher
    82/Suzanne and Nick Geary 70